The Calm Kitchen

The Calm Kitchen

LORNA SALMON

ILLUSTRATIONS BY NAOMI ELLIOTT

National Trust

First published in the United Kingdom in 2021 by
National Trust Books
43 Great Ormond Street
London
WC1N 3HZ

An imprint of Pavilion Books Company Ltd

ISBN 978-1-91165-702-6

A CIP catalogue record for this book is available from the British Library.

10 9 8 7 6 5 4 3 2 1

Reproduction by Rival Colour Ltd, UK
Printed and bound by Toppan Leefung Ltd, China

This book is available at National Trust shops and online at www.nationaltrustbooks.co.uk, or try the publisher (www.pavilionbooks.com) or your local bookshop.

CONTENTS

Introduction   6
Storecupboard essentials   8

SPRING   10
SUMMER   38
AUTUMN   70
WINTER   100

Thank You   126
Index   127

INTRODUCTION

'Let food be thy medicine and medicine be thy food.'
HIPPOCRATES

We've never been so distanced from our food and where
it comes from. Our lives have never been so hectic, so
influenced by technology, so commodified. We find ourselves
with less and less time to invest in nourishment, of both our
bodies and our minds. Nutrition, exercise, rest – these are,
generally, the first things to fall by the wayside, particularly if,
like me, you can find yourself struggling with the stresses and
anxiety that seem to come hand-in-hand with modern life.

The Calm Kitchen is more than just a recipe book. Following
the four seasons, it's a beginner's guide to reconnecting with
nature through food as a form of self-care, from the soothing
smell of lavender in summer to the simple magic of baking

a loaf of bread on an autumn evening, from shopping (or foraging) for your favourite seasonal ingredients to cooking them to feed yourself or your friends and family.

I want to share with you how mindful cooking, baking, foraging and feasting (the latter being my personal favourite) can lead to better peace of mind, health and well-being. I'll take you through a collection of foolproof recipes alongside informative, insightful guides to ingredients and how they can benefit your physical and mental health. You will also find tips on foraging across the hundreds of miles of countryside, woodland, orchards and kitchen gardens in the United Kingdom, including some of my choice favourites in the National Trust's care.

I can't really begin to describe quite how much spending time calmly cooking and baking has benefited my mental health – but for you, I'm going to try.

Oven temperatures given are for fan ovens. If you use a conventional oven you may need to increase the temperature by 10°C.

STORECUPBOARD ESSENTIALS

These are the essential ingredients I'd be lost without. All of which, unsurprisingly, feature in the recipes throughout this book.

I derive unbridled joy from unpacking and putting away 'the big shop'. I find it so calming and therapeutic to stack the various tins, pour grains and pulses into glass jars (a great way to keep track of what needs restocking, with the added side benefit of making your worktops look beautiful), and watching the shelves in the fridge burst into shades of green, red and orange.

Just looking at all the fresh fruit, vegetables, grains and pulses I've gathered to cook makes me feel healthy and brings me joy – and that's half the battle, right?

So, here are my *Calm Kitchen* storecupboard essentials:

TINNED FOODS

- Tomatoes – try to go for plum over chopped as they're usually higher quality
- Kidney beans
- Butter beans
- Borlotti beans
- Baked beans
- Chickpeas
- Artichokes – less faff than fresh

GRAINS, PULSES AND PASTA

- Basmati rice
- Arborio rice
- 'Soup' pasta – orzo, ditalini
- Pearl barley
- Spaghetti
- Split red lentils
- Rolled oats
- Plain flour
- Self-raising flour
- Wholemeal flour
- '00' flour (for pasta)
- Semolina

HERBS AND SPICES (DRIED)

- Salt
- Black pepper
- Vegetable stock cubes/ bouillon
- Basil
- Oregano
- Thyme
- Rosemary
- Paprika

- Smoked paprika
- Ground cumin – seeds are even better
- Ground coriander
- Ground cinnamon or cinnamon sticks
- Garam masala
- Turmeric

MISC.

- Tomato purée
- Baking powder
- Bicarbonate of soda
- Eggs – ideally free-range and local

- Olive oil
- Extra virgin olive oil
- Soya mince

SPRING

Delicate blossom forming on trees, little green hints of new growth scattered over naked branches and clear blue skies: I welcome with open arms the optimism that's gifted with the first days of spring, the season that's about new leaves and deciding which ones to turn over. New beginnings, a fresh start. Now, I don't know about you, but I couldn't possibly do anything before I've had some brunch.

ESSENTIAL SPRING PRODUCE

(and why it's good for you)

PEAS Peas contain vitamins K, C and A, needed for bone-building, blood coagulation and to support your immune system, as well as being a top-notch source of plant-based protein.

ARTICHOKES Artichokes are rich in folate (vitamin B9), which is essential for making red blood cells. They're also a good source of minerals like calcium, potassium and iron.

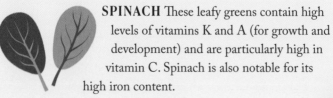 **SPINACH** These leafy greens contain high levels of vitamins K and A (for growth and development) and are particularly high in vitamin C. Spinach is also notable for its high iron content.

ASPARAGUS A good source of vitamins K, C, A and E, asparagus also contains a hearty helping of folate, which helps to make healthy red blood cells.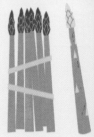

WATERCRESS Watercress has long been hailed as a 'superfood'. It's an incredibly nutrient-dense food – it's full of vitamins C and K and per gram has more iron than spinach.

JERSEY ROYAL POTATOES

These are a source of vitamin C as
well as complex carbohydrates,
which are essential for maintaining
energy in a longer-lasting and more
stable way.

SPRING ONIONS An unsung allium hero, spring onions
are loaded with antioxidants, such as vitamin C. You'll also find
a healthy dose of vitamin K.

CHARD Eating chard can help you to maintain
healthy blood pressure. It is an excellent source of
vitamins K, A and C, as well as a good source of iron,
magnesium and potassium.

RADISHES Red radishes are full of potassium
and calcium, which is good for healthy bones
and teeth, as well as immune-boosting vitamin C.

Full Springlish

Best enjoyed on that first bright, sunny morning of spring alongside a cup of fragrant Earl Grey tea with a squeeze of fresh lemon. This meal is a celebration of spring vegetables – with one of my all-time favourites taking centre stage: the mighty asparagus. This is my hero ingredient of spring, in no small part because of its enlivening flavour and distinctive texture. Seeing the vibrant, fresh greens of the asparagus and baby spinach next to the cheerful yellow egg yolks in this dish is bound to put a smile on anyone's face – and that's before you've even tasted it.

Serves 2

250g asparagus spears
extra virgin olive oil
4 very fresh free-range eggs
2 English breakfast muffins
1 tbsp salted or unsalted butter
2 tbsp shop-bought green pesto or Pestle and Mortar Pesto
  (see page 53)
100g baby spinach
4 sprigs freshly chopped flat-leaf parsley
Parmesan, pecorino or vegetarian Italian-style hard cheese
  (optional)
salt and freshly ground black pepper

1 Have a look at your asparagus spears – you might want
to remove the ends as they can be quite woody. I find it
particularly enjoyable to carefully bend the spears to find
the point where they break naturally, then snap off the ends
– this mindful motion is so satisfying. Don't rush to throw
the ends in the composter as they can be saved for the Orzo
Verde on page 31. Cook the asparagus in boiling salted water
for 3–4 minutes or until just tender.

2 Drain the asparagus and put into ice-cold water, so it doesn't
lose its lush green colour. Drain again and toss in the fruitiest
extra virgin olive oil you have, then season to taste and set aside.

3 Choose a saucepan that's large enough to accommodate all
4 eggs comfortably. Fill it with lightly salted water and bring

to a simmer over a low to medium heat – avoid the water becoming too bubbly, as this will disturb the eggs and cause them to separate. Once the water is simmering, crack the eggs into the pan, holding the shell as close to the water as you can, allowing for a little 'breathing room' between each egg (ideally 5mm–1cm). For a runnier poached egg, cook for just 3–4 minutes until the white is set. Cook for a further 2 minutes if you prefer your yolks less runny. Remove one by one using a slotted spoon, then drain on kitchen paper.

4 Split and toast the muffins, and top them in this order: butter, a layer of pesto and a handful of fresh spinach.

5 To serve, lay the asparagus on top of your buttery, pesto-topped muffins. Add the poached eggs, then sprinkle over a little parsley. Finish with black pepper and some cheese shavings, if you wish.

FOOD AND THE FIVE SENSES

The sights, the smells, the textures ... Before you even taste the ingredients that you plan to use in your meal, connecting with your food in this way is an act of mindfulness.

We tend to focus on just one sense when we think about food – taste. Yet the other four senses are involved in not only the pleasure of eating but also the joy of cooking. If we mindfully engage these as we prepare and eat our food, we can get even greater enjoyment from it. Not only that, but it's also an act of thanks and respect to the growers who've worked so hard to get the produce on to our plates. If you've ever tried to grow your own vegetables, you'll understand the trials and tribulations that come with it – and just how proud a moment it is when your efforts finally make it to the dinner table.

As we continue on our journey through spring, I encourage you to try your hand at picking out all of these details in your fresh ingredients. What do they smell like? How will your prep impact their texture and flavour? Considering these questions will place you firmly in the present as you prepare your meal. Let's explore this a little further together.

SIGHT We've all heard the phrase, 'first, we eat with our eyes'. Often, this is the first sense that's engaged as we select our produce. Food shopping can often be quite a manic experience, with the key aim being to hurry through the shop as quickly and efficiently as possible. The next time you visit your local shop or farmers' market, try to appreciate the variety of colours in the different fruits and vegetables. What change can you see from unripe to perfectly plump and ready to eat? Pick out as many different colours as you can – consider how these foods can complement each other visually, as much as through their flavours.

TOUCH Get into the habit of picking up fruits and vegetables when you're choosing them – a firm, green mango isn't the best choice if you want it for dessert that evening, so find one that gives slightly beneath your thumb. As you prepare your food, enjoy the sensations of slowly peeling an orange, snapping off the woody ends of asparagus, washing mud from potatoes and rubbing butter into flour with your fingertips for scones. The simplest, seemingly everyday tasks of food preparation are acts of mindfulness in the kitchen. Slow down and consider these processes, and how they make you feel – aside from making your tummy rumble, that is …

SMELL If sight is the first sense to be engaged, smell is a close second. This sense is crucial to our pleasure in food – if we lose our sense of smell, we often lose our ability to taste, too. I'm going to go out on a limb here and say you've walked into the house before and have been greeted by the smell of sizzling onions and garlic. My Achilles heel

is the smell you get on the approach to a bakery. I can pick out all the different elements: ground coffee, sweet pastry, freshly baked bread straight from the oven. Smell is evocative of moments in time, and very often strongly linked to fond memories. What's your most vivid food memory, by smell?

SOUND We touched on this slightly with smell (see what I did there?). Think tipping potatoes into scorching hot oil as you prepare a roast dinner, tapping the bottom of a loaf of bread to check that it's cooked (if it sounds hollow, you're good to go); even when you're not the one in the kitchen, you can hear the clattering of saucepans, the stirring of sauces, and if you're in my house – the tapping of dancing feet. This all combines into the pleasure of anticipation as food is prepared.

TASTE Last, but not least, and this one's a biggie … taste. Little else compares to that satisfying moment of tucking into a dish you've poured your love and time into. I might sound like a broken record here, but now more than ever – slow down. Consider each and every flavour. It was worth adding that extra half-teaspoon of cumin, right? That combination you dreamed up on the spot really worked – it's just a little hint of rich, dark chocolate coming through there … Take the time to mull over your meal, perhaps even think how you'll make it bigger and better next time – or better still, after much thought and a few extra bites, realise it's perfect just as it is. Next time you sit down for a meal, turn off any and all digital distractions, leave your phone in another room, lay the table (no matter how big or small), shut your eyes and really taste it.

Vibrant Watercress Soup

Watercress is another foodie treasure found during spring. Hailed as a 'superfood', watercress is nourishing, wholesome and full of antioxidants. I enjoy it in many ways – a simple handful on the side of a fresh pasta dish or stirred through a risotto in lieu of my usual spinach to give a peppery kick. In this classic recipe, however, the watercress is bold, and the soup is so satisfying in its simplicity to make.

TIP Get creative with the garnishes and add one or more of the following: a swirl of cream or crème fraîche, a twirl of pesto or extra virgin olive oil, some toasted flaked almonds or croutons, a few pea shoots or chopped chives.

Serves 2

1 tbsp olive oil
4 spring onions, finely chopped
1 small–medium potato, peeled and cut into 1cm cubes
600ml hot vegetable stock
80–100g watercress
salt and freshly ground black pepper

1 Heat the oil in a large saucepan, add the spring onions
and cook gently for 4–5 minutes until soft, and then add the
potato and cook for a further 5 minutes, stirring occasionally.

2 Add the stock and bring to the boil, then reduce the heat
and simmer for 15–20 minutes until the potato is soft.

3 Stir in the watercress, reserving a few sprigs to garnish, and
simmer for 3–4 minutes. Using a hand-held blender or food
processor (whichever you have or find easiest), whizz the
soup until smooth.

4 Season to taste with salt and black pepper and serve
in warmed bowls. Top each with the reserved sprigs of
watercress. Serve with Wild Garlic and Cheddar Scones
(see page 24).

FORAGING FOR WILD GARLIC

Wild garlic is one of the highlights of spring. If you've never foraged before, wild garlic is a brilliant place to start as it's widely available and easy to identify, not only by its shape and size, but – surprise, surprise – by its scent. It is known by a variety of different names: devil's garlic, stinking jenny, ramsons, wood garlic, broad-leaved garlic, buckrams. I have to say my personal favourite is 'bear's garlic'.

There's a plethora of well-being benefits connected to foraging. First and foremost – you're out in nature, getting involved. Foraging engages your senses – what can you see, what can you smell, did you just spot a deer scarper off into the undergrowth? Being out in nature is a wonderful salve for a busy mind, and equally brilliant for your physical health.

Now, where do you find wild garlic? I'd recommend not foraging from the roadside, given the pollution kicked out by vehicles. Aim for shady, wooded areas – you'll find swathes of it sprawled across the forest floor, winding its way through the tree trunks, flecked with the whites of its star-like flowers.

There are two different types of wild garlic, *Allium ursinum* and *Allium triquetrum*, with the former being the most common. A foolproof test to confirm you do indeed have wild garlic: crush the leaf in your hand. If it smells like garlic, you've hit the jackpot. Choose the longest, brightest and greenest leaves you can find as these will be the tastiest.

Most National Trust outdoor sites allow sustainable foraging for personal use, personal being the key word here! Make sure that it's plentiful in the area you're taking it from, and only ever take what you plan to eat. Also check that you aren't crushing any underfoot as you select your chosen shoots. Be sure not to pull the wild garlic you find out of the ground, bulb and all. Not only will this mean they won't return to be enjoyed next year, but you'll also be in breach of the Wildlife and Countryside Act (1981), which protects all wild plants.

You can get incredibly creative with wild garlic in the kitchen – try Wild Garlic and Cheddar Scones (page 24) and Pestle and Mortar Pesto (page 53). You can also knead it into a basic white cob loaf, add strips to salads or stir through a pasta sauce ... anywhere you might find garlic, really!

There are all sorts of places across the UK where you'll be able to forage wild garlic. This is where the National Trust website really comes into its own, so get searching for your local foraging spots! It also has invaluable safety information. Here's where to find it: nationaltrust.org.uk/outdoors.

Wild Garlic and Cheddar Scones

When I've been out foraging for wild garlic, this is my tried and triple-tested go-to recipe to share with friends. If you can't find any wild garlic, or you're reading this out of season, fear not – you can easily substitute a finely chopped garlic clove and some spinach, or a handful of fresh chives (10g will be enough).

This recipe gives me the chance to introduce you to one of my favourite kitchen utensils: the mezzaluna. It's a handy herb chopper – a half-moon-shaped blade with two little handles either side. Not only is it fun to say, it's another way to engage in mindfulness in your kitchen. For the full effect, you need to use it on a mezzaluna board with a shallow indentation. It makes the chopping of fresh herbs and garlic effortless: you rock the blade back and forth in a rhythmic fashion, and before you know it, you're ready to season your meal.

Makes 4 (or 6 × 6.5cm round scones)

225g self-raising flour, plus extra for dusting
60g butter, cubed
50g foraged wild garlic leaves, thoroughly washed
70g cheddar cheese, grated (I usually use extra mature),
    plus extra for topping
½ tsp salt
½–1 tsp coarsely ground black pepper (optional)
80ml semi-skimmed milk
1 medium free-range egg

1 Preheat the oven to 180°C fan/gas mark 5. Lightly oil a baking sheet.

2 Sift the flour into a large mixing bowl, then add the cubed butter. Get in there with your hands and, working quickly and lightly, rub the ingredients together between your fingertips. Not only is this hugely satisfying, but it's what will give you that essential scone texture. Stop when the mixture resembles breadcrumbs.

3 Chop your wild garlic – I use my mezzaluna (see opposite) for this.

4 Mix the grated cheese and wild garlic together, then add to your scone mixture, together with the salt and pepper. (If you're not a huge fan of pepper, you can omit this – if you love it, you can add more later with the final topping of cheese.)

5 Pour 60ml of the milk into a measuring jug and crack the egg into it. Whisk together, using a fork. Slowly pour this into the dry ingredients, then mix together with a wooden spoon until fully combined into a ball of dough.

6 Dust a clean work surface with flour and pop the ball of dough onto it. Flatten it (either by hand, or using a rolling pin) until it is about 2cm thick, then cut it into four equal pieces. If you'd prefer your scones to look a little neater, use a standard (6.5cm) biscuit cutter, or failing that a glass tumbler, to cut out circles of dough.

7 Dip the top of each scone in the remaining milk, then top with a little grated cheese. Bake for 15–20 minutes (I always check after 10–12 minutes to see how they're getting on). You want the scones to be a beautiful golden colour.

8 Leave on a wire rack to cool just long enough so that they're safe to handle – and by handle, I mean dip into that delicious watercress soup you prepared earlier (see page 20).

TIP This recipe is a perfect way to practise mindfulness in the kitchen. Tactile acts like rubbing butter into flour, kneading dough, and even stirring a sauce help us to engage with the cooking process, and connect with the ingredients we're using.

Jersey Royal Aloo with Cashews and Cucumber Raita

What I love about making Indian food is how artfully every herb and spice is considered. I'd always been daunted by cooking that involves a multitude of different ingredients, but really, it's all about practice, getting to know each one and what they add to your meal. You'll be surprised how quickly a spice you've never heard of becomes a staple. My most-used Indian spices include the ever-popular turmeric (for colour, as well as its antioxidant benefits) and cumin (which is naturally rich in iron). I also use plenty of garlic, the wonder allium.

This main and side showcase just how light and fresh Indian cuisine can be. You can make all sorts of switches with

27

the ingredients to fine-tune the recipes to your own taste. If you like it spicy, add more chilli. Want slightly sweeter tomatoes? Then a teaspoon of sugar will help. The raita really couldn't be any easier to make – there's no cooking involved, so you can whip this up while the curry is bubbling away.

Serves 2

250–300g Jersey Royal potatoes, scrubbed
1 tsp ground coriander
1 tsp garam masala
½ tsp ground turmeric
½ tsp ground cumin
1 tsp caster sugar
juice of 1 lemon
2–3 tbsp vegetable oil
4 spring onions, finely chopped
3 cloves garlic, finely chopped
1 green chilli, deseeded and finely chopped
½ × 400g tin plum tomatoes or 200g fresh ripe tomatoes, chopped
100g unsalted, whole cashews
200g fresh spinach, trimmed and roughly chopped

Cucumber raita
250g plain full-fat yoghurt
1 cucumber, cut in half
1 tsp ground cumin
handful of fresh mint leaves, torn (optional)
salt and freshly ground black pepper

1 Fill a saucepan with salted water and set over a medium heat. Add the potatoes and cook for 15 minutes until a knife can be easily inserted into them. Drain the potatoes, reserving a mugful of the cooking water. Depending on their size, cut them in half or into quarters and leave the smaller ones whole.

2 In a small bowl, stir together the spices, sugar, lemon juice and 2–3 tablespoons of water – I use some of the water that I used to cook the potatoes.

3 Heat the vegetable oil in a large, heavy frying pan – ideally cast-iron – over a medium-high heat. When hot, add the potatoes and fry for 5–8 minutes, turning occasionally, until golden brown all over. Once golden, remove the potatoes and set aside.

4 Reduce the heat to medium, adding a little more oil if needed, add the spring onions and cook until they start to turn golden; add a splash of water if they begin to stick. Add the garlic and chilli and turn the heat to low, otherwise the garlic will burn and produce a bitter taste. Cook for 4–5 minutes to allow the flavours to combine.

5 Now add the spice mixture and stir for a few minutes until most of the water has evaporated. Add the chopped tomatoes and simmer for another 5 minutes or until your tomatoes have thickened nicely.

6 To make the cucumber raita, pour the yoghurt into a bowl. Grate the cucumber over the yoghurt – you may only need half the cucumber, but we all like different consistencies, so add it to your liking. Stir in the cumin and a sprinkling of salt and pepper to taste, along with half of the fresh mint. Again, add more or less as you see fit – if you want a punchier raita, add another ½ teaspoon of cumin. Top with the remaining fresh mint.

7 Add the cashews to the curry and stir. Stir in the spinach a few handfuls at a time, waiting until each handful wilts before adding another. Cover and simmer for about 5 minutes, stirring occasionally.

8 Remove the lid, stir in the potatoes and season with salt. Cook for another 5 minutes to heat the potatoes through.

9 Serve with fragrant basmati rice and the cooling cucumber raita.

TIP The joy of cooking from scratch is that it allows you to tailor recipes to your own taste. Once you've mastered a recipe from this book, try dialling up and down certain elements. Add an additional clove of garlic, try a squeeze of lime instead of lemon. Before you know it, you'll know your taste buds like the back of your hand.

Orzo Verde

I hate wasting anything in my kitchen, so I'm always seeking out new ways to make use of all the fresh produce I buy. Asparagus is a classic springtime example, and this recipe uses all of the asparagus spears by boiling and blending the ends to incorporate into the bright green sauce.

I use orzo in this recipe, but you can also use other classic Italian 'soup' pasta such as ditalini or macaroni – whatever you have in your storecupboard, really.

Serves 2

150g orzo
200–250g asparagus spears
200g frozen peas
1 vegetable stock cube
½ tbsp dried oregano
½ tbsp dried basil
200ml boiling water
30g Parmesan, pecorino or vegetarian Italian-style hard cheese, grated
handful of salad leaves or baby spinach (optional)
salt and freshly ground black pepper

1 Bring two saucepans of salted water to the boil. Pour the orzo into one and cook for 8–10 minutes. Once cooked, drain in a sieve (not a colander as it might fall through the larger holes), then rinse in cold running water (this will remove the starch and stop it sticking together). Leave to drain well.

2 Break off the woody ends of the asparagus and add them, along with the rest of the asparagus spears, to the other saucepan of boiling water; cook for 3 minutes. Drain well and then pop the woody ends into a food processor or blender. Tip the rest of the asparagus into a bowl of ice-cold water to stop the cooking process and 'set' its bright green colour; when it's cold, leave to drain well.

3 Add the frozen peas, vegetable stock cube and dried basil and oregano to the food processor, then pour over the boiling water. Leave for around 10 minutes to 'cook' the peas and cool slightly. Do NOT blend before the peas have had a chance to cool, as the lid will fly off, causing a great big mess. Trust me on this one.

4 Once your sauce ingredients have cooled, whizz them up until they form a lush, green sauce.

5 Return the cooked orzo to the pan, add the sauce and the rest of the asparagus, and warm over a medium-low heat for 3–4 minutes.

6 Serve the orzo topped with grated cheese and a handful of crunchy salad or spinach leaves if you wish.

Bramley Apple Cranachan

This dessert was inspired by recent memories of staying in a converted shepherd's hut on the Isle of Skye. To some, sunbathing on a beach is heaven. To me, it's sitting in the armchair of that rickety little hut enjoying a comforting bowl of cranachan.

Cranachan is a traditional Scottish dish, usually made with raspberries, and whenever I'm eating it, it transports me back to this time and place. We can't always be in our most comforting, nest-like spots, but what we can do is relive them through mindful acts in the kitchen. Food, and our memories of it, allow us to travel back to certain moments in time. I encourage you to think of a time and place when you felt content and at peace – and recreate the food or drink you were enjoying in that moment.

I use Bramley apples for this recipe. It's safe to say they're the reigning queen of cooking apples, but any juicy, acidic apple you can get your hands on will do the trick. I've chosen heather honey as an homage to Scotland, but you can also use a local honey – you really can't go wrong.

Serves 4

2 Bramley apples
100g rolled oats
2 tbsp golden caster sugar (or light brown sugar),
   plus 1 tsp for the cream
pinch of ground cinnamon
2 tbsp heather honey, plus extra for drizzling (optional)
250ml double cream
2 tsp vanilla extract (or 2–3 tsp whisky if you're feeling naughty)
granola (optional)

1 Put a 500ml Kilner jar (or other largish jar) in the freezer before preparing your other ingredients (I'll explain later!).

2 Peel, core and finely dice the apples. Put the apples and 4 tablespoons of water in a saucepan over a medium heat. Cover and cook for 15–20 minutes, or until the apples are soft enough to be mashed with a fork. Check regularly and add a further tablespoon of water if the mixture looks dry.

3 While your apples are cooking, warm a frying pan over a medium heat. Add the oats, sugar and cinnamon and cook for 4–5 minutes, stirring frequently, until the oats are nicely toasted. Leave to cool.

4 Roughly mash the cooked apples together with the honey.

5 Remove the jar from the freezer, pour in the cream, vanilla extract (or whisky), and a teaspoon of caster sugar, seal the jar and shake for about 3–5 minutes. And … ta-da! As if by magic, you've got thick whipped cream.

6 Take four glass jars or large tumblers, and add to each jar the toasted oats, followed by the apple purée and then the whipped cream.

7 You can drizzle over more honey and top with some granola if you wish.

Elderflower Cordial

One of the best things about elder is that it isn't picky about where it grows; you're just as likely to find a shrub cascading over a fence down a city alleyway as you are on a woodland walk. Elderflowers bloom from late May until the end of June, and are easy to identify – you're looking for sprays of fluffy white flowers standing on top of several proud, straight stems. If you aren't sure, give it a sniff: the freshest elderflowers have an almost creamy, floral scent. Snip off your chosen blooms, give them a shake to remove any bugs (this is instead of washing; if you wash them you'll lose all the delicious pollen) and store them in a freezer-proof container. I rarely make my cordial as soon as I get home with my loot, so often opt to freeze them and use at my leisure.

Before you start this recipe, make sure you have some sterilised bottles for storage (see page 99). I like to use smaller bottles and I tend to share them around with friends as I go a bit wild with picking elderflowers. I buy citric acid from my local independent chemist, but you can also get it online; I'd recommend checking the likes of souschef.co.uk or buywholefoodsonline.co.uk. If stored in properly sterilised bottles in the fridge, this cordial should keep for several months.

Pour a little of the cordial over ice in a glass and top up with cold water or sparkling wine or, if you're planning on enjoying your cordial in colder months, try topping it up with hot water and adding a strip of orange zest for a warming treat.

Makes 1 litre

2 unwaxed lemons
900ml boiling water
1kg granulated sugar
20 elderflower heads
20g citric acid

1 Use a vegetable peeler to pare off the lemon zest in strips, then slice the lemons and set aside.

2 Pour the boiling water into a large saucepan, add the sugar and stir until it has fully dissolved, then immediately remove from the heat.

3 Throw in the sliced lemons and zest, elderflower heads and citric acid. Give it a good stir, then cover with a clean tea towel and leave for at least 12 hours or overnight.

4 The following morning, line a colander with muslin and pour through some boiling water. Place the muslin-lined colander over a wide jug or bowl with a pouring lip and strain the cordial through the muslin; it may take 20 minutes to drip through but don't leave it too long. Pour the cordial into sterilised bottles and keep in the fridge.

SUMMER

When summer arrives, it's with a kaleidoscopic
bounty of colours, scents and flavours.
Summertime means togetherness in the great
outdoors; a time for sharing. The evocative
sensations of summer have inspired these recipes,
from the smell after rainfall on a hot day to the
enlivening freshness of mint, and the fruit … oh,
the fruit! I hope they will help you relive those
fond memories of past summers.

ESSENTIAL SUMMER PRODUCE

(and why it's good for you)

STRAWBERRIES Strawberries are highly nutritious as well as being delicious, and their vitamin C, folate (vitamin B9) and potassium contents are where they really shine.

RASPBERRIES Small but mighty, raspberries contain a wide variety of vitamins and minerals including vitamin K. And in just one serving (100g), you'll get 50 per cent of your daily vitamin C intake.

BLACKCURRANTS Blackcurrants pack a powerful nutritional punch for something so small. They contain vitamins A and E, but they're actually richest in vitamin C. Thanks to this, they're fantastic for giving your immune system a boost.

REDCURRANTS Redcurrants, unsurprisingly, have similar benefits to blackcurrants. They're equally rich in vitamin C, with a small portion (60g) providing 40 per cent of your daily allowance. They're particularly tart, mind, so I tend to opt for a smaller portion!

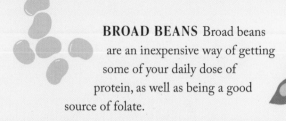

BROAD BEANS Broad beans are an inexpensive way of getting some of your daily dose of protein, as well as being a good source of folate.

AUBERGINE Aubergines are a good source of vitamins B1 and B6. Our bodies aren't able to store the former, so it's important to include it in your diet.

RED PEPPERS Red peppers are full of antioxidants and contain a sizeable helping of your daily vitamin C intake, as well as being a reliable source of vitamin B6.

TOMATOES Tomatoes are best known for their vitamin content, which includes beta-carotene (which becomes vitamin A when eaten), vitamins C and E, some B vitamins and vitamin K. They're also one of the easiest things to grow at home as a budding gardener.

ROCKET Fresh rocket is rich in folate, as well as being an excellent source of vitamins A, C and K. This peppery salad leaf packs a real punch!

Raspberry and Basil
Scotch Pancake Stacks

This is a real crowd-pleaser that showcases one of my most
summery, grow-your-own-inspired flavour combinations.

Serves 4–6/Makes 20 pancakes

400g raspberries
40g granulated sugar
450g self-raising flour
1 tsp baking powder
½ tsp salt
600ml buttermilk
3 large free-range eggs, separated
50g melted butter, plus extra for cooking
1 tsp vanilla extract
4–6 sprigs of fresh basil leaves (1 sprig = 3–4 leaves), torn
100g mascarpone or Greek yoghurt

1 Put half the raspberries in a small saucepan, add the sugar and cook over a medium-low heat for about 5 minutes until it has thickened slightly but is still saucy. Pour into a bowl and set aside – this will be your raspberry sauce.

2 Sift the flour, baking powder and salt into a large bowl.

3 Put the buttermilk, egg yolks, melted butter and vanilla in another large bowl and beat with a balloon whisk or a fork until evenly mixed. In a third, clean glass bowl, whisk the egg whites until stiff.

4 Make a well in the centre of the dry ingredients, pour in the buttermilk mixture and whisk together. Add a large spoonful of the egg whites and stir in with a metal spoon to loosen the batter a little. Fold in the remaining egg whites, preserving as much air as possible, until you have a thick, fluffy batter.

5 Heat a frying pan over a medium heat and melt a little butter. Pour about half a ladleful of batter into the pan to make each pancake (you should be able to make two or three at a time), along with a few torn basil leaves – the smell will linger on your fingers in the most delightful way.

6 Cook for 2–3 minutes, until the pancakes are golden brown on the bottom and firm enough to flip (you should just about be able to see that they are cooked through beyond halfway), turn them over quickly and cook for a further minute or two on the other side. Transfer to a plate, or keep them warm in a low oven, while you cook the remaining batter in the same way.

7 To serve, top the pancakes with a hearty tablespoon of mascarpone or Greek yoghurt, along with some of the raspberry sauce. Finally, scatter over some fresh raspberries and a little more basil.

MINDFUL KNEADING

If you asked my friends and family which bread I bake the most, they'd undoubtedly say my rosemary and sea salt focaccia (see page 47 for the recipe). Why? Well, aside from it being a moreish slab of salty, carby goodness, the whole process of preparing, baking and then eating my very first focaccia helped trigger my 'eureka' moment. It showed me how much of a salve cooking, and particularly baking, was for my mental health. Having been diagnosed with generalised anxiety disorder and depression while at university, I've always been in search of coping mechanisms that I can turn to on tougher days. After what felt like years of searching, the answer had been in front of me all along.

Breadmaking forces you to be present. It demands your attention. It draws your focus into the very moment you're in – shaping, pushing and pulling the dough – I find the rhythmic quality of it so relaxing. It's like yoga but you get a freshly baked loaf at the end of your practice (the dream).

Bread tells you to slow down. I'm not sure if you've ever tried to rush through the breadmaking process, but I would highly recommend that you don't. I've put loaves in the oven after proving them just once to see if I could get away with it. I didn't. I've turned up the heat just a 'smidge' to hurry things along. Guess what? It was perfectly burnt. I've even forgotten to add yeast before and wondered why on earth my bread didn't rise.

Bread can be wily, and this can put people off right from the get-go. But I've never seen a smile quite like the one you see on a person's face after they've baked their first successful loaf of bread. It's the best thing since, well …

Now, don't get me wrong. The times it has gone wrong have ruined the next hour or so of my life. But the ones that have gone right – after plenty of trial, error and flour-covered kitchen floors and aprons – have made it all worth it. It's a brilliant demonstration of what you can achieve in the kitchen, and indeed, life, if you're brave enough to just take that first step. Yes, you might not get it quite right the first time, or the second … but what about the third?

So, you'll generally find me at the end of a stressful week, kneading dough, chopping vegetables, stirring sauces, tasting, dancing, singing (sorry, neighbours). Our house might be unusual, in that my partner and I tend to fight over who's cooking most nights, for this exact reason. We get joy from cooking – the joy of being present, perhaps for the first time that day, and sharing that joy with another person.

Rosemary and Sea Salt Focaccia

This focaccia recipe is a firm favourite in my house. There's a lot to love about it. In particular, once you've nailed this version, you can get really creative with your toppings and flavours. I've made a sun-dried tomato version, as well as a more autumnal walnut and truffle oil variation. This bread also travels very well (be it in a bike basket or backpack), making it ideal alongside a salad as part of a summer picnic.

Focaccia is one of my favourite breads for a variety of reasons. Firstly, you knead it in oil, which is the loveliest and most satisfying feeling. It's a sensory experience – the squelching noises, the fragrant scent of olive oil, the rich, golden dough slowly absorbing the flavours. My recipe makes two small loaves, which ties into one of the recurring themes of summer for me: sharing. One for you, one for a friend. I'm not a huge fan of rules, but that's one I'll always stick to when making focaccia.

Makes 2 small loaves

500g strong white (bread) flour
2 tsp sea salt, plus extra for sprinkling
7g fast-action dried yeast
2 tbsp olive oil, plus extra for oiling
300ml lukewarm water
bunch of fresh rosemary, divided into small sprigs
fruity extra virgin olive oil

1 Put the flour, salt, yeast, olive oil and water in a mixing bowl. Using your hands, bring the ingredients together and knead the dough in the bowl for 3–5 minutes.

2 Tip the dough onto a clean work surface greased with some olive oil and knead the dough for a further 5 minutes. When kneading, use the heel of your dominant hand to push the dough away from you, then roll it back in on itself and give it a quarter turn. Keep doing this until you can feel the dough becoming more pliant. You'll soon find a rhythm to this, moving the dough back and forth, back and forth …
Add more oil when the dough begins to stick to your work surface. This adds to the depth of flavour of the focaccia, and also makes for some delightful noises.

3 Put the dough in a lightly oiled bowl. Cover with a tea towel and leave in a warm spot to prove for 1 hour, or until doubled in size. I prove my bread in the oven on a very, very low heat – no more than 30°C. If you do this, be sure to leave your oven door open.

4 Line two baking trays with baking parchment. Divide the dough into two. Shape each piece into an oval about 2.5cm high, place on the baking trays and leave to prove in a warm place for a further hour.

5 Preheat the oven to 200°C fan/gas mark 7.

6 Using your thumb or pinched fingers, dot your dough with holes, a few centimetres apart. Fill the holes with fresh rosemary sprigs, then drizzle over some more olive oil (your fruitiest extra virgin). Be generous with this – it will pool in the holes and soak into your bread as it bakes. Sprinkle all over with sea salt and bake for 15–20 minutes until golden brown.

7 Leave the focaccia to cool on top of a wire rack. Focaccia is best enjoyed on the day it's baked, while still a little warm, but it tastes just as good the day after.

TIP If you don't think you'll eat both in one sitting, you can keep the other loaf in the freezer for up to a month. Take it out of the freezer the day before you plan on eating it so it can defrost naturally overnight – avoid microwaving it at all costs because this will ruin the loaf and some parts will become very chewy and unappetising. Once defrosted, pop it back in the oven at 200°C fan/gas mark 7 for 10 minutes, so it will be warm and smell freshly baked again.

TIP This loaf is designed for tearing, sharing and dipping. I'll often bring the dynamic flavour-packed duo of dukkah and pesto (see pages 51–53) to accompany my focaccia at picnics. You can repurpose either a 250ml Kilner jar or a clip-top jar to store and safely carry your dips to your picnic without spillages. As the dukkah is dry, you'll also need to bring along some extra virgin olive oil – either in its bottle or poured into another jar. Dip the focaccia into the oil and then into the dukkah so that the herbs and spices stick to the loaf. The more oil on your bread, the more dukkah you get! For the pesto, either dive in and dip, or simply spread over your bread for maximum coverage.

Dukkah

Dukkah is a fragrant spice mix originating from Egypt, and one that has fast become a staple in my cupboard right next to the salt and pepper. It has a crunchy texture and is good sprinkled over soups and salads as well as eaten with bread and olive oil. If you have lots of little glass storage jars, I'd highly recommend doubling the quantities below and making some more to enjoy later. Homemade dukkah will last for up to a month in an airtight container.

Makes 1 jar (about 350g)

75g hazelnuts or walnuts

2 tbsp sunflower seeds

1 tsp fennel seeds

1 tbsp cumin seeds

3 tbsp coriander seeds

3 tbsp white sesame seeds

1 tsp coarse sea salt

½ tsp freshly ground black pepper

2 tbsp black sesame seeds

1 tsp nigella seeds (kalonji)

1 Gently dry fry the nuts and sunflower seeds in a pan for 3 minutes. Transfer to a blender, spice grinder or – my personal favourite for this – a pestle and mortar.

2 Add the fennel, cumin, coriander and white sesame seeds to the pan and dry fry for 2 minutes.

3 Add to the blender or grinder and pulse a couple of times, or if you're using the pestle and mortar, a few grinds should do it. You're looking for small pieces that keep their crunchy texture, not a powder.

4 Add the sea salt, pepper, black sesame seeds and nigella seeds and give the mixture a final quick blitz or grind to combine.

5 Store the dukkah in an airtight jar. Use it to intensify soups, dips and salads or treat yourself to focaccia dipped in olive oil and dukkah at your next picnic.

Pestle and Mortar Pesto

This is the simplest pesto recipe I've ever made, and it works like a charm. It's a little bit of a workout, too, so you'll have more than earned it.

If you have a large mortar, you can double this recipe and add it to soups and risotto. Make sure you store your pesto in an airtight container, covering the top with a layer (about 5mm) of extra virgin olive oil, and it will keep for up to a week. Not that it generally lasts that long in my house, mind.

Serves 4

30g pine nuts, toasted
50g basil leaves
1 clove garlic, peeled
about 100ml extra virgin olive oil
50g Parmesan, pecorino or vegetarian Italian-style hard cheese, grated
salt and freshly ground black pepper

1 Put the pine nuts, basil and garlic into a mortar and mash it all together with the pestle. Keep going until the ingredients form a paste.

2 Pour in the olive oil, add the grated cheese and mix together. Season to taste.

Duck Egg Shakshuka with Burrata

Since eating my first burrata at one of my favourite local brunch spots, I've not been able to stop. It fits perfectly with this recipe as, when torn, the creamy cheese combines with the rich tomato sauce. I like to serve this shakshuka in a sharing dish with a loaf of fresh bread for dipping – turning it into more of a 'brinner' (brunch for dinner) in our house.

The duck eggs in this recipe have deep orange yolks, which add a glorious pop of colour. Plus, they bring a rich, creamy taste that never goes amiss. This dish works just as well with free-range chicken eggs, but if you feel like trying something a little different, now's your chance!

Serves 2

olive oil

1 onion, chopped or sliced

2 red peppers, deseeded and sliced

1–2 cloves garlic, finely chopped

1 tsp ground cumin

1 tsp smoked paprika

400g tin chopped tomatoes

2–4 free-range duck eggs

1 burrata, drained

3–4 sprigs fresh coriander, roughly chopped

salt and freshly ground black pepper

1 Preheat the oven to 160°C fan/gas mark 4.

2 Heat a glug of olive oil in a heavy-based, ovenproof frying pan over a medium heat. Add the onion and red peppers and fry gently for 10–15 minutes until soft.

3 Add the garlic, cumin, smoked paprika and tomatoes and simmer for 10–15 minutes, so the sauce thickens slightly. Season to taste with salt and pepper.

4 Using a wooden spoon, make four wells in the tomato sauce, then break an egg into each as quickly as you can, so that they cook evenly.

5 At this point, to make it extra-indulgent, I add a drizzle of olive oil over the top, and then put the frying pan in the oven.

The cooking time depends on how you like your eggs – start at 5 minutes if you prefer a runnier egg, and test the top of one egg very softly with a knife: you should see/feel the yolk move slightly. If you prefer a firmer yolk, cook them for 8–10 minutes.

6 To serve, top with half a burrata per person and a good sprinkling of coriander. Oh, and don't forget a hearty chunk of fresh, crusty bread for the all-essential dipping.

TIP Don't worry if you don't have an ovenproof frying pan – you can cook the eggs the traditional way, on the hob. Cover the pan with a lid to help the eggs cook.

Artichoke and Broad Bean Risotto

I love artichokes – they're so beautiful, hugely versatile, and
I always have a jar or tin of them in the cupboard. This is
one of those dishes that I'll put together towards the end of
the week when we're running a little low on fresh vegetables
in the fridge. It makes great use of both storecupboard and
frozen goodies and proves that you don't need the freshest of
greens to create a well-rounded, nutritious meal.

Serves 2–3

1 tbsp olive oil
½ onion, finely chopped
2 cloves garlic, chopped
40g unsalted butter
1 tbsp dried basil

1 tbsp dried oregano

200g arborio rice

100ml dry white wine

750ml–1 litre hot vegetable stock

150g frozen broad beans

200g tinned or jarred artichokes, drained and sliced in half
  or quarters

40g Parmesan, pecorino or vegetarian Italian-style hard cheese,
  grated (optional)

2 sprigs of fresh basil (one for each serving)

salt and freshly ground black pepper

1 Heat the olive oil in a large saucepan (you'll be doing a lot of stirring!). Add the onion, half the garlic, half the butter and the dried herbs. Let them get their sizzle on until the onion has softened slightly. Now it's time to add the rice. Stir the onion and herbs through the rice, coating it evenly with butter – you want to see the rice become glossy before you take the next step.

2 Crank up the heat just a little and pour in the wine. It'll make the most satisfying noise and fill the room with a gorgeous smell. Continue to stir the rice until the wine has nearly evaporated. Once most of it has been absorbed by the rice – which will look very shiny, almost translucent – start adding your hot stock.

3 Make sure you add the stock a ladleful at a time, stirring frequently and waiting until it has been absorbed before adding the next ladleful. Patience. This is the sort of meal that can't be rushed, so enjoy the slowness of the cooking process. Once you've used half of the stock, add the remaining garlic, the broad beans and artichokes, then continue adding the rest of the stock, stirring in a ladleful at a time, until it has all been used. Your risotto is done when the rice is al dente – with a little bite to it – the sauce will be creamy and reasonably loose. This should take around 25 minutes.

4 Add the remaining butter, along with most of the grated cheese – saving just a little to add on top when serving. Stir the cheese through well, then serve promptly, topped with a sprig of fresh basil. Sprinkle over the remaining cheese but don't be shy about grating more over the top if this doesn't look cheesy enough for your taste buds!

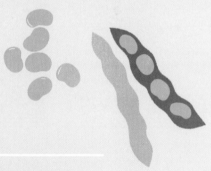

TIP You can add some of my Pestle and Mortar Pesto (see page 53) as a show-stopping extra if you wish. I like to take a teaspoon, dip it into the pesto sauce, then dangle the spoon over the bowl – dotting the risotto with flecks of resplendent green.

Blackcurrant and Mint Sorbet

This recipe lends itself perfectly to being made at a leisurely pace at the start of the week with the aim of enjoying it at the weekend. It's one of those 'Oh, this is just something I threw together …' kinds of dishes to impress your guests. I'll look ahead to the weekend weather and if the sun is set to shine, that's my cue to source some local blackcurrants.

To freeze your sorbet you'll need a 1-litre freezer-proof container – I'd advise using a metal container if possible, as this will help the sorbet to freeze more quickly. Once frozen, you can transfer your sorbet to an airtight container and store it in the freezer for up to a month. Any longer than that, and you might find ice crystals begin to form. That's if you don't eat it all in one sitting!

Serves 4-6

250g caster sugar
200ml water
20g fresh mint leaves,
    plus 4–6 sprigs, to serve
900g blackcurrants
2 tbsp freshly squeezed lemon juice
100–120g summer fruits, to serve
    (20–30g per person)

1 Put the sugar, water and mint in a saucepan and heat gently, stirring frequently, until the sugar is fully dissolved. Leave to cool, allowing the mint to infuse for at least 20 minutes. Once cool, strain through a fine sieve.

2 While the syrup cools, purée the blackcurrants in a food processor, then strain through a fine sieve or squeeze through a piece of muslin to remove the seeds – or simply rub them through a fine sieve, which is harder work to begin with, but achieves the same result: seed-free purée.

3 Add the cooled syrup and the lemon juice to the blackcurrant purée.

4 Pour the mixture into a 1-litre freezer-proof container and pop it in the freezer. Every 30–40 minutes, remove the sorbet from the freezer and give it a good stir with a fork. Make sure you finish by levelling the mixture. Once you have repeated this a few times, it will firm up. This will take 3–4 hours.

5 To serve, use an ice-cream scoop to spoon your sorbet into bowls, ideally white ones, as they'll really make the rich, dark colour of the sorbet pop. Top with a sprig of mint leaves and a sprinkling of fresh summer fruits.

STOP AND SMELL THE LAVENDER

Lavender is often celebrated for its de-stressing qualities, so it should be no surprise to see it featured in a book about finding calm through cooking. Its evocative smell is effortlessly relaxing – due in no small part to the amount of it we like to use in bubble baths, and the droplets we might add to our pillowcases to aid a restful night's sleep. When it's in full bloom in summer, I always try to press and dry fresh lavender for the winter months. I use it bunched up in natural cotton drawstring bags among my clothes, or preserve it as flavoured sugar (particularly useful for my shortbread recipe, see page 64) to remind me of longer, warmer days.

The famous phrase might encourage us to 'stop and smell the roses', but the same could equally be said of lavender. Not only the scent but the sight of lavender dancing loftily in the breeze as it's courted by bustling bumblebees brings me such joy.

The most famous English variety is 'Hidcote', a name which might ring a bell for those of you as obsessed with wandering around summer gardens as I am. The National Trust garden at Hidcote, nestled in the very north of the Cotswolds, was the life's work of garden designer Lawrence Johnston and became famous for its lavender, which can be seen there to this day.

I'm not about to compare my tiny urban garden to Hidcote, but I've taken a little bit of Hidcote and its lavender home with me, and allowed the place to inspire my own garden. I've divided my space into seasonal sections, with bursts of colour rising up and falling with each week and month. The left side is neatly kept and well-planned, the right, well ... I've left that for nature to do her thing. It's overgrown, overrun, a total mess – and full of life.

I'm pleased with just how easy it was to introduce lavender and bring all its sensory delights home with me. What's fantastic about it is that it doesn't matter how big or small your garden might be or, indeed, whether you have one at all. It's equally at home in a pot on a balcony as it would be in a garden border – it's not super-fussy, making it an ideal plant for a first-time gardener.

Lavender bridges the gap beautifully between the garden and the kitchen, with each sharing mindful qualities that I've reaped the benefits of over the years. I've been a cook for far longer than I've been a gardener, but the two skills complement one another wonderfully. On my toughest days, I've downed tools at my desk and wandered into the garden to idly check on how my bulbs are doing or whether the French beans need watering (again). It taps into my need to care for things.

The mental health benefits of cooking really do extend beyond the kitchen and into the great outdoors that provides the ingredients – be it a city centre garden, or an orchard in Gloucestershire. All that matters is how we learn to embrace and celebrate what we have.

Lavender Shortbread

During summer you can take advantage of the fresh, local lavender found throughout the UK. It's worth noting that this recipe will also work without the lavender as a classic, plain shortbread, but raspberries or blueberries make wonderful alternatives. Simply whisk 50g fresh raspberries or blueberries into the butter in place of the fresh lavender.

Makes 20–24 small biscuits

125g unsalted butter, softened, plus extra for greasing
1 tbsp freshly picked lavender flowers
70g caster sugar
175g plain flour, plus extra for dusting
25g demerara sugar

1 Put the butter and lavender into a mixing bowl and beat together using a balloon whisk – or a hand-held electric whisk, which will speed up the process considerably! Whisk for 3 minutes – you'll know you've whisked enough when you can smell the lavender releasing its calming fragrance.

2 Beat the caster sugar into the lavender butter, then stir in the flour until it's evenly mixed. Be careful not to over-work the dough or you will undo all the brilliant work you did whipping together the butter and lavender, and your shortbread texture will be too firm once cooked.

3 Dust your work surface with flour, keeping the flour nearby in case you need to sprinkle over a little more. Divide the dough in half and gently roll each piece into a cylinder 10–15cm long: the dough is rather fragile at this stage, but don't worry, it will firm up in the fridge. Cut two pieces of baking parchment large enough to wrap the dough. Sprinkle the demerara sugar over the parchment and gently roll the dough in the sugar until evenly coated. Wrap and chill for 30 minutes – overnight is also fine – until firm enough to slice.

4 Preheat the oven to 140°C fan/gas mark 1 and lightly grease two baking trays or line them with baking parchment. While the oven is warming up, slice the dough into rounds, 1–1.5cm thick, and place on the prepared baking trays, leaving space for the biscuits to spread.

5 Bake for 15–20 minutes until the shortbread is pale golden brown at the edges. Carefully lift the biscuits on to a wire rack and leave to cool completely. This is perhaps the hardest part for me because I always want to eat them immediately, but it's worth the wait as they become crisper when they're cold.

TIP Try to remember to freeze some lavender so you can enjoy this fragrant and relaxing shortbread during those deep, dark nights of winter. Freeze lavender flowers in small bags, or freeze the lavender-infused butter made in the first step of this recipe, shaped into a log. Frozen lavender butter will keep for up to 6 months.

Raspberry Iced Earl Grey

I always make sure to have a batch of this refreshing
drink ready in the fridge if the weekend weather forecast
looks set to stun.

Serves 4–6

1 orange
500g raspberries
3 sprigs of mint
4–5 tsp runny honey
5 Earl Grey teabags
1 litre water

TIP If you don't have orange peel, you can also use
the peel of most citrus fruits. I've used lemon peel
before, and it cuts through the sweetness of the
honey beautifully.

1 Use a vegetable peeler to pare off the orange zest in strips. Put the raspberries in a jug and crush with a wooden spoon.

2 Add the orange zest, mint, honey, teabags and water and stir well. Cover and place in the fridge for at least 6 hours or overnight, to allow the flavours to mingle and infuse.

3 Remove the teabags and mint sprigs. Pour the tea and raspberries through a fine mesh strainer and gently rub the raspberries to push through some of the fruit while leaving the pips in the sieve. Serve over ice.

Damson Lemonade

Make the most of early-ripened damsons in late summer. Forage and cook your damsons immediately or freeze to use in autumn and winter. This recipe also preserves your damsons in liquid form so you can enjoy them for many months ahead.

Makes 1 litre

12 damsons (fresh or frozen)
60g granulated sugar
400ml water
juice of 4 lemons, plus slices to serve
sparkling water, to top up

1 Put the damsons, sugar and water in a saucepan over a medium heat to make a syrup. Gently crush the damsons to help release the colour, and stir until the sugar has completely dissolved – you'll stop feeling its crunchy texture against the spoon you're using to stir, and the mixture will begin to thicken. This should take 3–5 minutes. The longer you leave the syrup over the heat, the thicker it will be, so don't do this for any longer than 5 minutes. If the sugar's not dissolving easily, increase the heat.

2 Once the sugar has dissolved, transfer the contents of the pan to a jug or a bowl with a pouring lip, ready to cool in the fridge. If you have the time, I'd recommend covering the bowl with a lid or a plate and leaving the flavours to infuse overnight. If you're strapped for time, 3–4 hours should do it.

3 Once cool, sieve the mixture into a large jug, add the fresh lemon juice, and top up with sparkling water. Treat it like you might cordial or fruit squash – you can always add more sparkling water if the flavour is too sweet or strong for you.

4 Serve immediately with ice and lemon slices.

TIP If you'd like to enjoy this drink later in the year, once cooled overnight you can strain the damson liquid into a 500ml Kilner jar and freeze it for up to 3 months. To serve, add the lemon juice and top up with sparkling water.

AUTUMN

Autumn is about watching the leaves turning to gold in front of your eyes. I love its slower pace and the chance to observe the change in seasons. Autumn is a season for reflection. We often career into it out of chaotically social summers, and it lets you breathe in, breathe out and pause. It's all about slowing down a little – and that being just fine.

ESSENTIAL AUTUMN PRODUCE

(and why it's good for you)

BLACKBERRIES Blackberries contain vitamins A, C and E. They're also a rich source of anthocyanins – powerful antioxidants that give the fruit their deep purple colour.

PEARS Pears contain vitamin C and calcium, which is very useful for keeping your bones and teeth healthy.

MUSHROOMS All types of edible mushrooms contain varying degrees of protein and fibre. They also contain B vitamins as well as selenium, which helps support the immune system. Buy wild mushrooms from the shops – foraging is for experts only!

CARROTS Carrots contain a variety of nutrients and antioxidants, along with vitamin C, which help to boost your immune system. They're also full of vitamin A, which is great for your skin.

APPLES The humble apple has so much to offer us nutritionally. Apples are a good source of vitamins A and C, both of which play a part in supporting our immune system. An apple a day …

BUTTERNUT SQUASH Butternut squash is a great source of vitamins A, C, E and B, and useful minerals such as calcium and potassium.

BROCCOLI Broccoli is very high in vitamin C and also contains many other vitamins and minerals including B6 and vitamin A. For a non-starchy vegetable, it has a good amount of protein, too.

CABBAGE The benefits of cabbage are quite similar to those of broccoli, given that they're in the same plant family. Cabbage is high in vitamin C, and incredibly versatile in the kitchen.

Hill Top Blackberry and Honey Flapjacks

This is my go-to 'breakfast on the go', which I always make using local Lake District honey from my hiking adventures there. The Lake District is well-known for one of its famous residents and farming champions: Beatrix Potter. Her home in Cumbria, Hill Top, is a must-visit for visitors from all over the world. You haven't really eaten a flapjack until you've enjoyed it atop a Cumbrian fell.

Makes 8–12 flapjacks

100g unsalted butter, plus extra for greasing
100g light soft brown or caster sugar
90g golden syrup
250g rolled oats
50g ground nuts, such as walnuts, almonds, hazelnuts or mixed nuts
250–300g blackberries
50g runny honey

1 Preheat the oven to 160°C fan/gas mark 4. Grease a 20cm square cake tin and line with baking paper.

2 Put the butter, sugar and golden syrup into a large saucepan over a low heat. Cook gently, stirring occasionally, until the sugar has dissolved.

3 Remove from the heat and add the oats and ground nuts; stir until the ingredients are evenly mixed. Tip two-thirds of the mixture into the prepared tin and press down firmly and evenly.

4 Mash the blackberries in a bowl, then stir through your honey and pour this over the flapjack base. Scatter the remaining oat mixture over the blackberries and gently press down to level the top.

5 Bake for 15–20 minutes until golden brown (they will be very soft at this stage), then leave to cool slightly before marking the flapjacks into pieces while they are still in the tin. Leave to cool completely in the tin before cutting into pieces.

Buttery Wild Mushrooms and Spinach on Toast

Having been vegetarian for most of my life, I've long been obsessed with mushrooms. Their variety and versatility is second to none and I'm quite proud of having turned some of my closest friends from mushroom haters to mushroom lovers. Above all else, be patient – don't be tempted to shake the pan around and stir them immediately because this is what makes them go slimy. Non-stick pans at the ready for this recipe, folks!

Serves 1

1 tbsp salted butter, plus extra for buttering the toast

1 large clove garlic, finely diced

100g wild mushrooms, such as chanterelles, morels or ceps
(or chestnut mushrooms if wild are unavailable), sliced

2 tbsp crème fraîche

1 tbsp freshly chopped flat-leaf parsley, plus extra to serve

handful of baby spinach

chilli flakes (optional)

salt and freshly ground black pepper

2 slices of toast, such as sourdough or Irish Soda Bread
(see page 79), to serve

1 medium egg, poached (optional), to serve

1 Put a non-stick frying pan over a medium heat, add the butter, then as soon as it has melted add the garlic and cook for 1–2 minutes. Add the mushrooms and cook for 3–4 minutes until golden brown, stirring very occasionally – be mindful not to move the mushrooms too much otherwise they will release liquid and become slimy.

2 Add the crème fraîche and parsley, season with a pinch of salt, then stir well and simmer for 30 seconds. Add the spinach, stir through, then remove the pan from the heat.

3 It's at this stage that you can add a poached egg if you fancy making the meal more substantial. You'll find my method for poaching an egg on page 14 in the Full Springlish recipe.

4 To serve, place the toast on a plate, butter liberally and top with the mushrooms and spinach. Garnish with a sprinkling of chilli flakes, if using, extra parsley and a hearty twist of black pepper.

TIP Alternative garnishes include switching the fresh parsley for thyme, adding a squeeze of fresh lemon or some crunchy croutons – the latter can be made from any leftover bread you might have lying around. Just divvy it up into 1cm cubes, drizzle with oil and bake for 8–10 minutes at 190°C fan/gas mark 6 until golden brown and crisp.

Irish Soda Bread

No kneading, no proving, no yeast. This is the bread to make if you've never made bread before. You'll get your hands messy as it's a wet dough, but that's all part of the fun! Traditionally buttermilk is used for this recipe, but my alternative version uses yoghurt and milk, which you're more likely to have in your fridge.

Makes 1 loaf

200ml low-fat yoghurt
60ml semi-skimmed or whole milk
1 medium egg
50g rolled oats
250g wholemeal flour, plus extra for dusting
1 tsp bicarbonate of soda
1 tsp salt
1 tsp caster sugar

1 Preheat the oven to 190°C fan/gas mark 6 and dust a baking tray with flour or line it with baking parchment.

2 Mix the yoghurt and milk together in a jug. Crack in the egg and whisk into the mixture.

3 Put the oats into a blender or food processor and blitz to a fine powder.

4 Put the flour, ground oats, bicarbonate of soda, salt and sugar in a large mixing bowl. Make a well in the centre and pour in the egg and yoghurt mixture. Bring the ingredients together with a fork, then use flour-dusted hands to shape the dough into a ball. The mixture will be a bit wet; add flour if necessary, to make it easier to handle.

5 Chuck the mixture onto the prepared baking tray and form into a rough circle. Don't worry too much if it's a little wonky, it adds to the rustic charm. Score a deep cross in the top using a very sharp knife. Bake for 25–30 minutes. Check your loaf after 20 minutes, turning it around so it bakes evenly. There's no yeast in this loaf, so it won't rise; don't worry, it's meant to be flatter than your standard loaf.

6 After around 25 minutes, using oven gloves, gently turn the loaf into your hand and tap the bottom – if it sounds hollow, it's done. (If not, put it back in the oven for 5 minutes or so.) Leave on a wire rack until cool enough to handle; it's best enjoyed when it's still warm enough for butter to melt when spread on top, or dipped into all sorts of scrumptious autumnal soups and stews.

TIP The loaf will keep for two days after baking and can be toasted and topped with the Buttery Wild Mushrooms and Spinach (see page 76).

Killerton Cobbler

This recipe uses smoked cheddar for the dumplings, and freshly milled flour from the National Trust's Killerton Estate near Exeter in Devon. It is my take on Josephine Ashby's Autumn Vegetarian Cobbler, as featured in the National Trust's *Veggie Comfort Food*.

If watercress reminds me of my birthplace in Hampshire, smoked cheddar reminds me of my other homeland in Bristol. This recipe is my love letter to the West Country and some of my most delicious finds from this beautiful part of the world.

Serves 4-6

2 tbsp olive oil
1 onion, finely chopped
2 tbsp mild paprika
1 butternut squash, halved, deseeded and cubed (peel, or leave the peel on for extra bite)
2 carrots, peeled and sliced
2 parsnips, peeled and sliced
1 small swede, peeled and cubed
400g tin borlotti beans, drained and rinsed
500g passata
2 tbsp muscovado sugar
1 tbsp chopped fresh oregano or 2 tsp dried
1 tbsp chopped fresh thyme or 2 tsp dried
2 tbsp tomato purée
salt and freshly ground black pepper

Dumplings
175g self-raising flour, plus extra for dusting
½ tsp salt
85g salted butter, diced
110g grated smoked cheddar cheese
2 tsp finely chopped fresh rosemary leaves or 1 tsp dried
2–4 tbsp water or milk

1 Heat the oil in a very large saucepan or flameproof casserole, add the onion and fry for 10 minutes until softened but not browned. Add the paprika, squash, carrots, parsnips and swede, stir well and cook for a few minutes. Add the borlotti beans, passata, sugar and herbs, and season with salt and pepper. Cover the pan with a lid and cook for about 30 minutes until the vegetables are tender. Stir in the tomato purée and add more seasoning if needed.

2 Meanwhile, preheat the oven to 190°C fan/gas mark 6 and make the dumplings.

3 Put the flour and salt in a mixing bowl and lightly rub in the butter with your fingertips until the mixture resembles breadcrumbs. Add two-thirds of the grated cheese and the rosemary. Stir in enough water or milk to make a thick dough.

4 Turn the dough out onto a floured surface and knead it lightly to ensure the ingredients are well mixed. Roll it into a circle about 2cm thick. Cut the dough into 5cm scones with a cup or knife or biscuit cutter if you have one, or simply cut the circle into 4–6 equal wedges.

5 If necessary, transfer the cooked vegetable mixture to an ovenproof dish. Arrange the dough pieces on top, brush with a little milk and sprinkle with the remaining cheese. Bake for 20–30 minutes until the topping is well risen and cooked through (test with a small pointed knife) and the cheese has melted.

THE JOY OF FEEDING
FRIENDS AND FAMILY

Cooking for people is one of my favourite things to do. It taps into a central pleasure I get from my relationship with food: sharing that love with others. I'll quietly squirrel away at a recipe behind the scenes, fine-tuning, testing and tasting before I decide my culinary creation is ready to be unveiled around the makeshift table in our flat's kitchen. It's a warm, comforting, safe space.

As someone who's been diagnosed with generalised anxiety disorder and depression, I can often find myself feeling low for no reason. At times I also struggle to put myself in social situations because they can be incredibly draining. But in recent years, I've noticed that food and friendship can have exactly the opposite effect. Especially when the two are combined: I feel restored.

The nature of my diagnosis means I have an inherently busy brain, and this is why the mindful act of cooking has been so beneficial for my health. I am, often for the first time during the entire day, forced to be present and focused on what I'm doing right here, right now. Distractions burn food. I am in my kitchen and this is my time. Not only for me, but for the loved ones I'm feeding that evening.

The self-care benefits of feeding friends and family are undeniable, and with that comes the pleasure of nourishing and sustaining others; all of which are amplified by the shared joy of eating and enjoying a meal together. Cooking

for others has genuine psychological benefits. In the most primal sense, our brain will reward us because we've successfully kept ourselves alive by eating. You're also reaffirming a powerful sense of community with your nearest and dearest. No wonder you feel so good after feeding not only yourself, but a room full of others! You are the provider, the caregiver, the nourishment-maker.

It was a revelation that something I'd been doing for so long was so beneficial for my mental well-being: the act of slowing down, going about my usual mindful meal prepping, chopping vegetables, stirring sauces and creating something delicious with my favourite music setting the pace for proceedings. That food then puts a smile on the face of the people you love most. I feel needed and loved in those moments – because I need and love them, too.

This is the joy of feeding friends and family – an age-old ritual designed to bring us all closer together, cementing relationships, laughing, reminiscing, celebrating. This happens around tables of different shapes and sizes across the world every day. Now isn't that a lovely thought?

Gnocchinese – Baked Gnocchi Vegetarian Bolognese

This dish has become a comfort food favourite. It's ideal to enjoy on a cosy autumn evening with friends; a tried and many times tested routine in our little Cambridge burrow. Use whichever mushrooms you like here – I tend to go for chestnut mushrooms as their hearty, earthy flavour adds real depth to this dish.

Serves 3–4

1 onion, chopped

2 cloves garlic, finely chopped

1 tbsp olive oil

250g chestnut or button mushrooms, chopped

1 tsp tomato purée

100g dried soya mince

500ml boiling water

1 vegetable stock cube

2 tsp dried basil

2 tsp dried oregano

400g tin plum or chopped tomatoes

500g fresh gnocchi

70g cheddar cheese, grated

100g mozzarella, torn

50g salad croutons

1 Preheat the oven to 180°C fan/gas mark 5.

2 Add the onion and garlic to a large ovenproof frying pan along with the olive oil and stir gently over a medium heat for 5–6 minutes until the onion has softened. Once softened, add the mushrooms, stir briefly to mix, then cook for 4 minutes, being mindful not to move the mushrooms constantly as this encourages them to release water and become slimy.

3 Add the tomato purée and stir. Then add the soya mince, a handful at time, along with some of the boiling water, stirring as you go. Once you have added all the soya mince, crumble in the stock cube and add the dried herbs.

4 Now, add the tinned tomatoes and stir again. Add more boiling water, as you will need some liquid to cook your gnocchi properly.

5 Once the sauce is bubbling away, add the gnocchi. Make sure you have enough sauce to completely cover it.

6 Pop the frying pan into the oven for 15 minutes, then remove and top with a mixture of grated cheddar, torn mozzarella and croutons for a satisfying crunch. (I have been known to use crisps instead of croutons, so don't be afraid to get creative.)

7 Pop the pan back in the oven for a further 20 minutes. It's ready when the top is deliciously golden and crispy, with a hint of bubbling sauce around the edges.

8 This dish is designed to be served as soon as it's come out of the oven, so make sure you have a generous salad or cooked green vegetable ready and waiting, and serve it pronto.

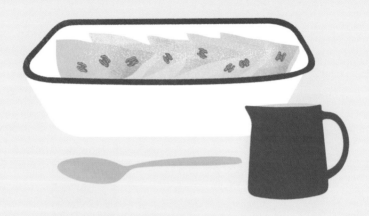

Pear and Walnut Bread and Butter Pudding

Summer isn't the only season with an array of delicious fruit to indulge in. Pears are an autumn classic and in this recipe they take their place in a favourite pudding. Just make sure your pears are fragrant and perfectly ripe (you may need to buy them three or four days before you need them).

If you're a particularly keen gardener and have the space, you might even consider growing your own pears. As with all fruit trees, make sure you know your soil and how much light your garden gets. I'd also recommend stopping by a local tasting event to see which variety is best for your needs.

Serves 4–6

4 slices of white farmhouse bread, crusts trimmed off, or brioche
    loaf (slightly stale is fine)
50–60g unsalted butter, softened, plus extra for greasing
3 ripe pears, peeled, cored and chopped into bite-sized pieces
40g walnuts, roughly chopped
40g demerara sugar, plus a little extra for sprinkling
3 medium free-range eggs
300ml whole milk
200g crème fraîche or 200ml double or whipping cream,
    plus extra to serve
1 tsp vanilla extract

1 Butter a 1.2–1.5-litre baking dish or roasting tin.
Butter the bread liberally and cut into halves or quarters
(depending on the size of the slices). Put a layer of bread in
the dish, then add the pears, most of the walnuts and half
the demerara sugar. Cover with another layer of bread.

2 In a large bowl, whisk together the eggs, milk, cream or
crème fraîche, the remaining sugar and the vanilla extract.
Once the sugar has been thoroughly mixed and you can
no longer see the granules, strain through a sieve over the
layered bread. Cover the dish with foil or a plate and set
aside for 30 minutes. At this stage, you can pop the dish
in the fridge if you're planning to cook it later. It really is
the perfect pudding to prepare in advance and serve with
a flourish later. If you want to cook it immediately, preheat
the oven to 160°C fan/gas mark 4.

3 Put the baking dish or tin on a baking sheet. Sprinkle the remaining walnuts and a little more demerara sugar over the top just before putting it in the oven. Bake for 25–35 minutes or until the top is nicely golden brown and the custard just set. Leave to cool for a few minutes, then serve with a dollop more crème fraîche or a little more cream.

Welsh Cakes

On a typically rain-soaked autumnal Sunday evening,
I looked in my cupboards to find I had exactly the
ingredients I needed to make these comforting little treats.

Makes about 16 cakes

225g self-raising flour, plus extra for dusting the surface
75g caster sugar, plus extra for dusting the cakes
½ tsp ground cinnamon
125g unsalted butter, cubed, plus extra for cooking
pinch of salt
75g sultanas or currants
1 medium egg
splash of semi-skimmed or whole milk (optional)

1 Sift the flour into a mixing bowl and add the sugar and
cinnamon. Add the butter and salt and lightly rub the
butter into the dry ingredients with your fingertips, until the
mixture resembles breadcrumbs.

2 Add the sultanas and mix in. Make a well in the centre of
the mixture and crack the egg into it. Whisk the egg with a
fork, then start to combine the ingredients. You might need a
splash of milk to bring the mixture smoothly together.

3 Transfer the dough to a floured surface and roll it out until
it's about 5mm thick. Cut out rounds using a 6.5cm biscuit

cutter. Smoosh the trimmings together, re-roll then cut out more cakes. Repeat until you've used all of the dough.

4 Heat a non-stick pan over a medium heat and after a few minutes, add a little butter to cook your first cake. After a minute or two, turn it and check its colour – depending on how dark it is, you'll need to adjust the heat. You want a warm golden brown. Once you're happy with the colour, turn it over and cook the other side for around 3 minutes.

5 Once your first Welsh cake has survived, cook the remaining cakes in batches – my pan fits about four at a time – for 2–3 minutes on each side.

6 Place the cooked Welsh cakes on a wire rack and dust both sides with lots of sugar. They taste the very best eaten immediately with a cuppa. Absolute sugary heaven!

BLACKBERRY-PICKING

While spring is all about foraging for wild garlic and
elderflower to use in sauces and syrups, early autumn
is often associated with finding one single, very special
hedgerow staple: blackberries. Blackberry-picking is an
evocative, immersive experience, so much so that it's been
the subject of poems by both Seamus Heaney and Sylvia
Plath (see 'Blackberry-Picking' by Seamus Heaney and
'Blackberrying' by Sylvia Plath). Each of these poems touches
on a particularly brilliant thing about blackberries: they will

seemingly grow anywhere and everywhere, be it an industrial alleyway paved with concrete in a bustling city, or a hedgerow in the deepest countryside full of bickering farmland birds.

Blackberry-picking is a mindful act, one that I enjoy most out in the forests nearest me, purely because I feel this amplifies the de-stressing nature of the activity. With the undeniable benefit that wild blackberries are, though smaller, more intensely flavoured than the cultivated ones, they are well worth seeking out. If you don't know where to find them, ask friends and family for their top tips. Local communities are always in the know with this sort of thing!

Blackberry-picking is also a great activity for getting little ones engaged in nature from a young age, often a pastime passed down from parents and grandparents, with the added bonus that the berries are easily identifiable, meaning there's little room for error, even for kids.

Here are my top tips for blackberry-picking:

- Wear jeans or thick trousers (ones you wouldn't mind getting covered in mud and thorns!) and a waterproof or thick jacket depending on the weather. The trousers and jacket will protect you from the thorns as you wade through the bushes to reach berries. It's also wise to bring gardening gloves, if you have some, so you can handle the brambles and carefully pick off the berries without spiking yourself. I have learned the hard way how useful gardening gloves are on these intrepid missions!
- As with wild garlic and elderflower foraging, make sure you pick your berries from as unpolluted an area as possible – so not a hedgerow that faces onto a busy road (which could

be quite dangerous due to the traffic, regardless). You'll also want to avoid low-growing fruit, which might have been subject to passing dogs …

- I've got into the habit of always bringing out a little container with me when I go on countryside walks. I'll often use old Tupperware – just make sure it is freezer-proof and seals properly and you're good to go.
- Bring a tall friend – or, failing that, something that you can use to knock the higher berries to the floor. At a mighty 5 foot 1, I rarely forage for blackberries alone for exactly this reason.
- As with any foraging, never pick more than you need. These berries aren't just for you – they're essential for wildlife at a time of year when nature's bounty isn't nearly as plentiful as in the spring or summer months.
- This one's very, very important – wash the blackberries before you eat them. You'll wash off any critters hitching a ride, as well as any foliage that won't be quite so delicious in your recipes. The centre should not be stained with juice, as this is an indication that there are worms inside.

Once washed, pop the blackberries in the fridge. You can eat them as they are, with yoghurt, over cereal or granola … Now they're wet, they'll go off a lot quicker, so freeze the rest if you aren't going to tuck in over the next day or two. You can then use your frozen blackberries in a plethora of recipes. I've been known to add them to an Eton mess when they've fruited earlier in the season, as well as puddings and crumbles. They also work well in preserves like jams, cordials (see page 98), and even cocktails. Bramble, anyone?

Blackberry and Vanilla Cordial

Cordial- and syrup-making are similar to breadmaking, in that once you've nailed the basic version, you can really let your creative juices flow. For example, once you've tried this recipe, why not switch out the blackberries for plums? Plums are in rich supply during autumn, and as with blackberries, they complement the vanilla used in this cordial.

I like to give my cordials to friends and family, so for this recipe I'd probably sterilise three 330ml bottles.

This recipe can be easily adapted to whichever season you're currently in. If you're leafing through during spring or summer, it works beautifully with tart raspberries or sweet strawberries.

Makes about 1 litre

1kg blackberries, rinsed and drained
1.5 litres cold water
500g granulated sugar
1 vanilla pod

1 Put the blackberries in a large saucepan and add the water. Bring to the boil and cook for 10 minutes. Strain the fruit into a clean bowl through a colander lined with a piece of muslin cloth or a clean tea towel, or a jelly bag if you have one. Leave it to drip for at least 4 hours, or ideally overnight. Don't be tempted to squeeze the mixture as it will make the cordial cloudy.

2 Return the juice to the cleaned pan and add the sugar and the vanilla pod (unsplit, as you don't want the seeds in the cordial). Heat gently and stir until the sugar has dissolved. Bring to the boil, then cook at a steady boil for 10 minutes, skimming off any froth on the top.

3 Remove the vanilla pod, rinse and dry for future use. Pour the cordial into sterilised bottles. It will keep for up to 3 months as long as you've properly sterilised your bottles.

TIP To sterilise bottles and jars, wash them in hot water with detergent, rinse thoroughly, then leave to dry in a very low oven, around 120°C fan/gas mark ½, for 20–30 minutes. Alternatively you can run them through the dishwasher on a hot cycle, or use a sterilising solution and follow the packet instructions. They should be thoroughly dried before use.

WINTER

Winter can be a tough time. The days are shorter, it's colder and it's most likely raining. We wake up in the dark, we come home in the dark. But I'm here to remind you of one of the very best things about winter: the food. Yes, winter can be long and dreary, but it's also indulgent, comforting and cosy. It's a time to rest, restore, revive – and feast with friends and family.

ESSENTIAL WINTER PRODUCE

(and why it's good for you)

BRUSSELS SPROUTS As with most green veggies, Brussels sprouts are full of vitamin K. They are also a great source of vitamin C and fibre.

CAULIFLOWER One serving (100g) of cauliflower has 100 per cent of your RDA of vitamin C. Move over, oranges! Cauliflower is also a good source of folate (vitamin B9) and vitamin K.

BEETROOT In beetroot you'll find plenty of calcium, iron and vitamins A and C, as well as a generous helping of folic acid, which helps our body produce and maintain new cells.

CELERIAC Celeriac is packed full of antioxidants and is high in vitamin C. You'll also find vitamin B6 and phosphorus, which works with calcium and vitamin D to maintain bone health.

CRANBERRIES Cranberries are a rich source of several vitamins and minerals, especially vitamin C, which is essential for the immune system.

ELDERBERRIES Hailed as an immune-boosting wonder-berry that's just perfect for consuming throughout the cold winter months, elderberries contain vitamins A and C, folate and even iron.

KALE It might be easier to list the things kale isn't good for! Appropriately named, it's a rich source of vitamin K, and also contains fibre, potassium and vitamin C, and it's high in antioxidants.

LEEKS Leeks are a good source of vitamins A, C and K. They also contain minerals like iron and manganese.

PARSNIPS Parsnips have an impressive range of nutrients including potassium, folate and vitamin C.

POTATOES Yes, potatoes really are good for you! They are a good source of vitamins C and B6.

SWEDE Swede has great health benefits and provides vitamin C, as well as being a good source of calcium and potassium. A winter staple!

Honey Walnut Porridge

Is there anything more comforting on an ice-cold morning than warming your hands around a bowl of porridge? Take a mindful moment to appreciate the warmth and flavours.

I've included the full recipe for my favourite version, as well as a selection of porridge-topper inspiration. Porridge oats are so affordable and it's really easy to add a bit of finesse with the click of a finger and a drizzle of honey. I use almond milk as I find this adds to the nutty flavours, but cow's milk or oat milk also works here. Or try using hazelnut milk for a more autumnal flavour.

Serves 4 (50g oats per person)

200g rolled oats
600ml milk of choice
500ml water
2 tbsp runny honey
¼ tsp salt
¼ tsp vanilla extract
½ tsp ground cinnamon
100g walnuts, crushed

1 Put all the ingredients, except the cinnamon and walnuts, into a saucepan. Stir well and simmer for 5 minutes over a medium heat, stirring often.

2 Serve with a spoonful of crushed walnuts and a sprinkle of cinnamon on top. If you prefer a more subtle cinnamon flavour, add it when your porridge is simmering. If you like, add a final drizzle of honey.

PORRIDGE TOPPING INSPIRATION

CHOCOLATE, BANANA AND ALMONDS Make your porridge extra-decadent by adding cocoa: replace the cinnamon in the recipe above with 1 tsp cocoa powder. Add sugar to taste, drizzle over some melted dark chocolate, then top with sliced banana and flaked almonds.

BANANA, DATES AND AGAVE Warming, spicy, sweet and filling. Add the cinnamon to the porridge while it is cooking, then top with some sliced banana, chopped dates and a drizzle of agave nectar.

CACAO NIBS, FLAXSEED AND PEAR This super-healthy topper packs a serious punch of goodness. Follow the recipe above, then sprinkle over some cacao nibs, flaxseed and chopped pear. I'll often add a big dollop of peanut butter on top too. This recipe is best enjoyed to refuel after morning exercise so you're set and ready for the day ahead.

Roast Root Vegetable Soup

My mum calls this 'Saturday Soup'. Why? Because it uses up all of the weekday vegetables you have in the kitchen that haven't been used up yet. Not only does it save on waste, it tastes absolutely delicious. Whenever I eat it, it makes me think of home.

Serves 4

200g parsnips, peeled and diced
200g swede, peeled and diced
250g carrots, peeled and diced
250g sweet potatoes, peeled and diced
4 tbsp olive oil
½ onion, diced
2 cloves garlic, diced
2–3 sprigs fresh rosemary or 2 tsp dried
2–3 sprigs fresh thyme or 2 tsp dried
1 litre hot vegetable stock
150g cabbage, sliced into strips (optional)
salt and freshly ground black pepper

1 Preheat the oven to 220°C fan/gas mark 7.

2 Divide the root vegetables evenly between two large baking sheets and drizzle liberally with olive oil, seasoning with salt and pepper as you go. Roast for about 30 minutes, shaking halfway through cooking so that they roast evenly.

3 Heat a large saucepan over a medium heat, pour in a glug of olive oil, then add the onion, garlic, rosemary and thyme. Season with salt and pepper and cook for 5 minutes, stirring regularly.

4 Add the roast root vegetables, followed by the vegetable stock, and give it a good stir to evenly coat the veggies. Bring to the boil, then reduce to a simmer, cover and cook for 5 minutes. Add the cabbage, if using, and continue to simmer for a further 5 minutes.

5 Remove from the heat and leave to cool a little. If your rosemary or thyme stalks look thick and woody, fish them out and discard. If you have a hand blender, blend to your chosen consistency. If using a food processor, wait until your soup is cool before popping the lid on and blitzing – it can get a bit messy if it goes in too hot.

6 Once blitzed to your desired consistency, return the soup to the pan and heat through when you're ready to serve. During the colder months, I always have this soup with a chunk of Irish Soda Bread (see page 79).

COMFORT FOOD

If there was ever a season for comfort food, it's winter.

Picture the scene. You've been caught walking home in the rain without an umbrella. You step in a gigantic puddle, only to realise there's a tiny little hole in your shoe that's now mercilessly letting in water. You really must get that fixed. The rain is not only falling downwards now, but sideways – meaning it can find you even if you have your hood up. Your feet are wet, your hands are wet, your face is wet. Not only is it freezing cold, but it's also dark because, if you hadn't been reminded enough already, it is winter.

But you turn the corner and home is in sight. The curtains are drawn, and you can see the warm glow of the living room lamp illuminating the window. You dig around in your bag, find your keys and step into the warm and dry at last. Rainwater drips from your not-quite-waterproof coat onto the floor around you, and you wonder where might be best to hang your drenched clothing. You feel tired, defeated and disgruntled, as one always does after an unfortunate trudge through the rain.

Then something magical happens. Could that really be the smell of dinner cooking? You pick out the ingredients and start to piece together the most delicious puzzle. The rich smell of slow-cooked tomatoes fills your nostrils, along with the intoxicating aroma of freshly baked bread. As you approach the kitchen, you're greeted by freshly torn basil. You've forgotten about that hole in your shoe and your almost-raincoat is a distant memory.

You're presented with a bowl of homemade soup to thaw your hands on, paired with thickly cut bread smothered in butter. The butter is melting slightly so you can be certain the bread has only just been baked. The soup bowl masterfully functions as a pair of gloves to accompany your well-worn and most trustworthy slippers. As you nestle into the corner of the sofa, a throw completes the look as it envelops you. Now you only need to listen to the rain from your nest. Everything is going to be okay.

Comfort food is safe and special. It's evocative and individual. I won't assume I know what yours is because it's so deep-rooted in our own memories, but I will be sharing with you some of my winter favourites. Think melted cheese bubbling and crisping. A square of the most intense dark chocolate. Fresh pasta coated in the earthiest of truffle oils. My comfort foods are quite firmly rooted in Italian cooking for the most part, no doubt because it's the cuisine that I grew up with. As you leaf through the pages of winter, I encourage you to think about your comfort foods, and relive the memories that made them special.

No-fuss Bean Chilli

This meal has been a lifesaver on many a winter's eve when it's hammering down with rain and I really don't fancy going outside for any additional fresh ingredients. I use a roasted red pepper because it adds a delicious sweetness, but if you want to use ingredients entirely from the kitchen cupboard, just leave it out. You can replace one of the tins of beans with baked beans: if you do that you won't need the sugar as they will contain sugar in one form or another.

Serves 4, generously

1 tbsp olive oil
1 onion, chopped
3 cloves garlic, crushed
1 roasted red pepper (optional), sliced
1 tbsp mild chilli powder
2–3 tsp smoked paprika
1 tsp dried oregano
2 x 400g tins chopped tomatoes
1 tbsp chipotle paste
1 tbsp sugar
400g tin kidney beans, drained and rinsed
2 x 400g tins black beans, drained and rinsed
freshly chopped coriander and soured cream, to serve

1 Heat the olive oil in a large saucepan. Add the onion and fry for 5 minutes until softened, then add the garlic and cook for another 2 minutes.

2 Add the roasted red pepper, chilli powder, smoked paprika and oregano and cook for another couple of minutes until the spices are fragrant. Add the chopped tomatoes, chipotle paste and sugar and bring to a simmer. Add the beans and cook for 20 minutes until the sauce has thickened.

3 Scatter over some coriander and serve with soured cream. As you can imagine, this dish also goes well with the rice variety of your choosing – if time allows, I always opt for brown basmati rice, as it adds a delicious nuttiness.

Mushroom Stroganoff

Stroganoff, like chilli, is an archetypal comfort food dish, rich and flavoursome. I like to serve it tossed with tagliatelle pasta, but you could serve rice on the side if you prefer. This recipe also makes good use of fresh flat-leaf parsley – one of our go-to windowsill herbs.

Serves 4

2 tbsp vegetable oil
1 onion, finely chopped
500g chestnut mushrooms, halved or quartered
4 cloves garlic, finely chopped
2 tsp tomato purée
1 vegetable stock cube
1–1½ tsp smoked paprika
3 tbsp light soy sauce
150ml crème fraîche
200ml boiling water
1–2 tbsp cornflour
300g fresh or dried tagliatelle pasta (see page 116 for a
    homemade version)
salt and freshly ground black pepper
roughly chopped flat-leaf parsley and grated extra mature
    cheddar cheese, to serve

1 Heat 1 tablespoon of vegetable oil in a large, deep frying pan or wok. Add the onion and fry for 2–3 minutes, stirring occasionally.

2 While the onion is browning, fill a large saucepan with water, add a generous pinch of salt and bring to the boil.

3 Add the remaining tablespoon of oil to your frying pan, followed by the mushrooms. Don't be tempted to move them too much, or they'll release water and become slimy; you want them to be golden and sealed, so turn very occasionally.

4 Once your mushrooms are golden, add the garlic and tomato purée and stir briefly, then crumble the vegetable stock cube over the top, add the smoked paprika and stir again.

5 Drizzle over the soy sauce, then stir in the crème fraîche. Slowly pour in the boiling water and season with salt and pepper to taste (it may not need much salt). Simmer for 4–5 minutes, ideally with a lid on, then check the consistency. If it's still runny, add 1 tablespoon of cornflour (mixed to a smooth paste with a tablespoon of cold water), then stir again. I like a reasonably rich, thick sauce, so I often end up adding another tablespoon of cornflour.

6 While your sauce is simmering, add the pasta to the saucepan of salted boiling water and cook until al dente.

7 Drain the pasta briefly – it should still be dripping water – add to the stroganoff sauce and mix well.

8 Divide between four bowls and top with chopped parsley and a generous grating of cheddar.

Fresh Tagliatelle

Winter nights give us more time inside and I've often found myself testing out new recipes during this time of hibernation. Plus, let's not forget the weather. Some evenings, I can't imagine anything worse than venturing out into the darkness and rain or snow for a bag of pasta. So, for those blustery winter nights, why not try making your own tagliatelle? The rule with pasta-making is easy to remember: 1 egg to every 100g of flour. You don't even need a pasta machine – though it would save a lot of effort when rolling out the dough. All you need is a fork, a rolling pin and a good sharp knife – perfect for beginners.

Serves 4

300g '00' or strong white flour, plus extra for dusting
3 medium free-range eggs
pinch of salt

1 Place the flour on a work surface and make a well in the centre. Crack in the eggs and add the salt.

2 Using a fork, gently beat the eggs and then gradually draw in the flour, a little at a time, until the dough comes together. If the dough is too stiff, add a little water, 1 tablespoon at a time; if too moist, add a little more flour.

3 Shape the dough into a ball, then start kneading it. Using the heel of your hand, stretch the dough away from you, then fold it back over itself and give it a quarter turn. Knead in this way for about 10 minutes until the dough is smooth.

4 Shape into a ball, place in a bowl and cover. Leave to rest in the fridge for 30 minutes (or up to 1 hour).

5 Turn the dough out on to a floured surface and divide it into three equal portions. Take the first portion (cover the other two with the upturned bowl), flatten it a bit and roll five or six times with a rolling pin. Give the dough a quarter turn and roll another five or six times. Keep rolling and turning until the dough is about 2mm thick. Repeat with the other two portions of dough. Leave it to dry (on a rack or clean towels) for 20–30 minutes or until it is no longer sticky, but still pliable.

6 Flour generously, then roll up into a loose cylinder. Slice the cylinder into strips about 7mm wide. Quickly unroll the strips and leave the tagliatelle to dry for another 5–10 minutes before cooking.

7 Bring a saucepan full of well-salted water to the boil and cook the pasta for 3 minutes until al dente.

MINDFUL WINTER WALKS

During these colder times when the days are shorter, we need to be even more mindful of how we're feeling, and to check in with ourselves and our loved ones more regularly. Sunshine is in short supply, so making the most of it when it appears is even more important. During these months, we tend to slow right down and enter hibernation mode. But winter really isn't all doom and gloom. For me, it can be quite the opposite, particularly when we're treated to clear, bright mornings. The sky takes on a cleaner, fresher quality, its pastel blue blended with a hint of the palest grey. It's expansive and inviting. On those days when there's not a cloud in the sky, you can see for miles – you can even see your breath.

Now's the time to embrace the saying: 'There's no such thing as bad weather, only unsuitable clothing.' Winter is for

woolly hats and walking boots. It's for scarves, gloves and a thick pair of socks. Winter is for walking.

The joy of walking is that it's an activity that many people can do, making it the perfect one to share with friends, family and children as a social activity, as well as one to do mindfully on solo expeditions. I tend to plan routes that are dotted with points of interest like waterfalls, viewpoints or, one of my personal favourites, a country pub pit stop. The latter is made particularly special if you're greeted by a roaring fire to warm your hands on or indeed, to dry your socks and gloves by!

Winter walks also provide an ideal opportunity for nature spotting, given the leaves have long disappeared from the trees. I won't claim to be a particularly brilliant birdwatcher, but some of my best spots have been during winter. To this day I remember when I saw my first ever treecreeper scurrying up a trunk in the Cairngorms National Park in Scotland. I was eating an oatmeal and raisin cookie at the time, so it was a doubly brilliant moment.

See, I did get to food eventually! I'm sure you never doubted me. Whereas summer is for barbecues, winter is the season of the flask. I tend to bring two with me – one will be full of tea, the other, soup. I am nothing if not prepared for my adventures, no matter how short or long I anticipate the walk to be.

I think that word sums up a winter walk for me – 'prepared'. Make sure you've got enough layers on to keep yourself at a comfortable temperature, always bring plenty of water and tea (the latter being absolutely essential, of course), make sure you have some portable snacks that will travel well (soup in a flask, flapjacks …), and most importantly, always, always make sure you have a dry pair of socks. Not every country pub will have a roaring open fire to save you, and I've learned that the hard way.

Hazelnut and Cranberry Brownies

This recipe is perfect when hosting friends or family or taking into the office to put a smile on your colleagues' faces. As this time of year is all about comfort food in our house, I tend to serve mine with a scoop of good-quality vanilla ice cream.

Makes 9 or 16 brownies

175g unsalted butter, plus extra for greasing

175g dark chocolate

250g caster sugar

1 tsp vanilla extract

3 large free-range eggs

85g plain flour, plus extra for dusting

3 tbsp cocoa powder

½ tsp salt

85g hazelnuts, roughly chopped

85g dried cranberries

1 Preheat the oven to 160°C fan/gas mark 4. Line a 20cm cake tin with baking paper.

2 Melt the butter and chocolate in a large heatproof bowl, set over a saucepan of simmering water, stirring occasionally until smooth. Remove from the heat and leave to cool until lukewarm – don't let it cool completely, or it will re-solidify.

3 Whisk in the sugar and vanilla extract. Next, whisk in the eggs, one at a time, until the mixture is glossy and smooth.

4 Sift together the flour, cocoa powder and salt, then sift again into the chocolate mixture and fold in. Fold in the chopped hazelnuts and cranberries.

5 Pour the mixture into the prepared tin, spreading it into the corners, and bake for 20–25 minutes. There should be a very slight wobble in the middle; the brownies will firm up as they cool. As hard as it might be, leave your brownies to cool completely before cutting into nine or sixteen squares (I sometimes sneak a little corner just to check it's not poisonous).

Chocolate Brioche Pudding

My indulgent, chocolatey winter twist on the classic bread-and-butter pudding, inspired by National Trust development chef Clive's springtime hot-cross bun and butter pudding.

Serves 4-6

unsalted butter, for greasing

6–8 chocolate chip brioche rolls (or a sliced brioche loaf)

75g chocolate hazelnut spread

75g dark chocolate, cut into small chunks

3 medium free-range eggs

250ml whole milk

100ml double cream or whipping cream, plus extra to serve (optional)

25g caster sugar

1 Grease a 1–1.2-litre baking dish with the butter.

2 If you're using brioche rolls, cut them in half and spread with chocolate spread. If you're using brioche loaf, slice it as if you're making yourself some toast and spread each slice with chocolate spread. Layer the brioche into your baking dish – you might need to halve some of your slices to fit. Sprinkle in the chunks of chocolate, then set aside.

3 Crack the eggs into a bowl and add the milk, cream and sugar. Use a fork or a whisk to whisk until fully combined, then pour over the brioche. Leave to stand for 30 minutes, so the brioche soaks up some of the delicious creamy mixture.

4 Preheat the oven to 160°C fan/gas mark 4.

5 Put the dish on a baking sheet (to catch any overflow as the brioche swell in the oven). Bake for about 30 minutes or until the custard has just set. Serve immediately, piping hot.

Elderberry Syrup

Hailed for its antiviral qualities, elderberry syrup can be served with soda water, as a hot drink, drizzled over porridge, or consumed by the tablespoon (or teaspoon for a child) as a winter boost for your immune system.

I've tried lots of elderberry syrup recipes and this one is geared towards my endless need for sweet, comforting treats during the winter months. Once I've foraged the berries in late September/early October I'll wash and then freeze them in whatever containers I have to hand. I'll make my first batch of syrup in November, to ward off winter coughs and colds.

I'm personally averse to cloves, which, for some, are an essential ingredient. With this in mind, I've tried to make my recipe as customisable as possible, listing all non-essential ingredients as 'optional'. Feel free to add them all if you want a punchy syrup with a traditionally festive flavour.

Makes 2 litres

600g elderberries

1.5 litres water

10 cloves (optional)

1 cinnamon stick (optional)

1 tbsp finely chopped ginger (optional)

70g runny honey

550g granulated or caster sugar

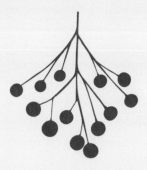

1 Strip the berries from their stalks, discarding as many of the stems as possible. Wash the berries and then put them in a large saucepan with the water. Add the cloves and cinnamon stick, if using, then bring to the boil. Reduce the heat and simmer for 30 minutes, gently mashing the berries to release the juice.

2 Stir through the ginger, if using, then drizzle in the honey. Line a colander with muslin and pour through some boiling water. Place the colander over a wide jug or a bowl with a pouring lip and pour the mixture through the muslin to remove the berry skins and any remaining stems. Return the juice to the cleaned pan and add the sugar. Heat gently and stir until the sugar has dissolved.

3 Pour the mixture into sterilised bottles (see page 99). Thanks to the sugar, this will last for up to 6 months – just make sure your bottles are properly sterilised!

THANK YOU

As someone who's meandered down the river of her mental health journey over the last ten years, I can honestly say that food, family, friendship and nature are what have helped me through the most – which is why writing this book has been so important to me.

To The Tall One, thank you for cheering me on and always believing in me while I wrote this. I can hear that you're cooking dinner upstairs, and whatever it is, it smells delicious. Thank you eternally for feeding the food writer.

To my parents and my big brother, thank you for teaching this little Salmon how to swim upstream.

To my Nan, Lucia, for providing me with the most wonderful set of pots and pans from your attic and perhaps the sturdiest marble rolling pin in the entire world. It's almost as strong as you are.

 Last but not least, my taste-testers extraordinaires across Cambridge, Surrey, London and Bristol – you've helped shape each and every recipe in this book. You're all so brave, and I love you very much.

INDEX

apples 73
  Bramley Apple
    Cranachan 33–5
artichokes 12
  Artichoke and Broad
    Bean Risotto 57–9
asparagus 12
  Full Springlish 14–16
  Orzo Verde 31–2
aubergines 41
beans
  Artichoke and Broad
    Bean Risotto 57–9
  Killerton Cobbler 81–3
  No-fuss Bean Chilli
    111–12
beetroot 102
blackberries 72, 95–7
  Blackberry and Vanilla
    Cordial 98–9
  Hill Top Blackberry
    and Honey Flapjacks
    74–5
blackcurrants 40
  Blackcurrant and Mint
    Sorbet 60–1
bread 45–6
  Irish Soda Bread
    79–80
  Pear and Walnut Bread
    and Butter Pudding
    90–2
  Rosemary and Sea Salt
    Focaccia 47–50
broccoli 73
brownies 120–1
Brussels sprouts 102
butternut squash 73
  Killerton Cobbler 81–3
cabbage 73

carrots 72
  Killerton Cobbler 81–3
  Roast Root Vegetable
    Soup 106–7
cashews: Jersey Royal Aloo
    with Cashews and
    Cucumber Raita 27–30
cauliflower 102
celeriac 102
chard 13
cheese
  Duck Egg Shakshuka
    with Burrata 54–6
  Full Springlish 14–16
  Gnocchinese 87–9
  Killerton cobbler 81–3
  Orzo Verde 31–2
  Pestle and Mortar Pesto
    53
  Wild Garlic and
    Cheddar Scones
    24–6
chocolate
  Chocolate Brioche
    Pudding 122–3
  Hazelnut and
    Cranberry Brownies
    120–1
comfort food 108–10
cranberries 102
  Hazelnut and Cranberry
    Brownies 120–1
cream: Bramley Apple
    Cranachan 33–5
cucumber: Jersey Royal
    Aloo with Cashews and
    Cucumber Raita
    27–30
Damson Lemonade 68–9

drinks
  Blackberry and Vanilla
    Cordial 98–9
  Damson Lemonade
    68–9
  Elderberry Syrup
    124–5
  Elderflower Cordial
    36–7
  Raspberry Iced Earl
    Grey 66–7
Dukkah 51–2
eggs
  Duck Egg Shakshuka
    with Burrata 54–6
  Full Springlish 14–16
Elderberry Syrup 124–5
Elderflower Cordial 36–7
feeding friends and family
    84–6
flapjacks: blackberry and
    honey 74–5
focaccia: rosemary and sea
    salt 47–50
foraging 22–3, 36, 95–7
Full Springlish 14–16
Gnocchinese 87–9
hazelnuts
  Dukkah 51–2
  Hazelnut and
    Cranberry Brownies
    120–1
honey
  Bramley Apple
    Cranachan 33–5
  Hill Top Blackberry
    and Honey Flapjacks
    74–5
  Honey Walnut Porridge
    104–5
Irish Soda Bread 79–80

kale 103
Killerton Cobbler 81–3
kneading 45–6
lavender 62–3
  Lavender Shortbread
  64–5
leeks 103
lemons
  Damson Lemonade
  68–9
  Elderflower Cordial
  36–7
mindfulness 17, 26, 45–6,
118–9
mushrooms 72
  Buttery Wild Mushrooms
  and Spinach on Toast
  76–8
  Gnocchinese 87–9
  Mushroom Stroganoff
  113–15
oats
  Bramley Apple
  Cranachan 33–5
  Hill Top Blackberry
  and Honey Flapjacks
  74–5
  Honey Walnut Porridge
  104–5
Orzo Verde 31–2
parsnips 103
  Killerton Cobbler 81–3
  Roast Root Vegetable
  Soup 106–7
pasta
  Fresh Tagliatelle
  116–17
  Mushroom Stroganoff
  113–15
  Orzo Verde 31–2
pears 72
  Pear and Walnut
  Bread and Butter
  Pudding 90–2
peas 12
  Orzo Verde 31–2

peppers 41
  Duck Egg Shakshuka
  with Burrata 54–6
  No-fuss Bean Chilli
  111–12
pesto
  Full Springlish 14–16
  Pestle and Mortar 53
porridge: honey walnut
104–5
potatoes 13, 103
  Jersey Royal Aloo
  with Cashews and
  Cucumber Raita
  27–30
  Vibrant Watercress
  Soup 20–1
radishes 13
raspberries 40
  Raspberry and Basil
  Scotch Pancake
  Stacks 42–4
  Raspberry Iced Earl
  Grey 66–7
redcurrants 40
risotto: artichoke and broad
  bean 57–9
rocket 41
scones: wild garlic and
  cheddar 24–6
seeds: Dukkah 51–2
senses 17–19
shortbread: lavender 64–5
sorbet: blackcurrant and
  mint 60–1
soup
  roast root vegetable 106–7
  vibrant watercress 20–1
spinach 12
  Buttery Wild Mushrooms
  and Spinach on Toast
  76–8
  Full Springlish 14–16
  Jersey Royal Aloo
  with Cashews and
  Cucumber Raita
  27–30

spring onions 13
  Jersey Royal Aloo
  with Cashews and
  Cucumber Raita
  27–30
  Vibrant Watercress
  Soup 20–1
storecupboard 8–9
strawberries 40
swede 103
  Killerton Cobbler 81–3
  Roast Root Vegetable
  Soup 106–7
sweet potatoes: Roast Root
  Vegetable Soup
  106–7
tea: Raspberry Iced Earl
  Grey 66–7
tomatoes 41
  Duck Egg Shakshuka
  with Burrata 54–6
  Gnocchinese 87–9
  No-fuss Bean Chilli
  111–12
walking 118–19
walnuts
  Dukkah 51–2
  Honey Walnut Porridge
  104–5
  Pear and Walnut Bread
  and Butter Pudding
  90–2
watercress 12
  Vibrant Watercress Soup
  20–1
Welsh cakes 93–4
wild garlic 22–3
  Wild Garlic and
  Cheddar Scones
  24–6
yoghurt
  Irish Soda Bread
  79–80
  Jersey Royal Aloo
  with Cashews and
  Cucumber Raita
  27–30